500 RECIPES
FOR PARTIES

500 RECIPES FOR PARTIES

Catherine Kirkpatrick

HAMLYN

Contents

Cover photograph by Paul Williams

Published by Hamlyn Publishing
Bridge House, London Road, Twickenham, Middlesex, England

© Copyright Hamlyn Publishing 1963
a division of The Hamlyn Publishing Group Limited

First published 1963
Fifth impression 1985

ISBN 0 600 32299 8

Printed and bound in Great Britain by R. J. Acford

Introduction

A good party begins from the moment when you sit down to plan it and although the keynote of entertaining today is informality, do be sensible about the size of the task you take on and do not deceive yourself about the amount of work and the expense involved in entertaining. Food should be simple – do not risk experimenting – and bear in mind when choosing your food the amount that can be prepared beforehand, the space in your kitchen and the capacity of your oven. Numbers are important too – it's only common sense not to invite 20 if there is only room for 12 to have a good party.

In this book you will find a host of exciting recipes and suggestions to try out on your friends and which suit every kind of party. There are 'working' menus too, which you can use as a guide, and you will find plenty of alternative dishes in the other chapters. A guide to quantities is given on page 48.

Invitations

For a formal party send a printed invitation card. This is also correct for a cocktail party—but you can use a simple 'At Home' card on this occasion. In both cases the details of time, date and address should be in your own handwriting. These invitations should be sent about a month in advance and call for a written answer.

An invitation to dinner should be by written letter. Short and to the point, giving details of time, date and place, it should be sent two or three weeks beforehand. For an informal party or to people whom you know well, a printed card with a gay design is suitable. Again it should be sent two or three weeks beforehand. Of course, there are occasions when invitations are given over the telephone, but although acceptable, this is not considered to be so courteous. Invitations to children should always be in writing.

No matter what kind of party you are giving, the first few minutes when your guests are arriving are the most important; in order that they will feel really welcome see that someone is detailed off to receive the guests. Decide where coats are to be put, and try to make sure there is a mirror available for last minute titivating. The use of a dressing table with spare tissues and a clothes brush is much appreciated—and make sure that everyone knows where the bathroom is. Above all—enjoy yourself. If you do—everyone else will, too.

In this book you will find suggestions and recipes for the food for every kind of party. There are 'working' menus too, which you can use as a guide, and you will find plenty of alternative dishes in the other chapters; a guide to quantities is given on page 48.

Some Useful Facts and Figures

Notes on metrication

In case you wish to convert quantities into metric measures, the following tables give a comparison.

Solid measures

Ounces	Approx. grams to nearest whole figure	Recommended conversion to nearest unit of 25
1	28	25
2	57	50
3	85	75
4	113	100
5	142	150
6	170	175
7	198	200
8	227	225
9	255	250
10	283	275
11	312	300
12	340	350
13	368	375
14	396	400
15	425	425
16 (1 lb)	454	450
17	482	475
18	510	500
19	539	550
20 (1¼ lb)	567	575

Note: When converting quantities over 20 oz first add the appropriate figures in the centre column, then adjust to the nearest unit of 25. As a general guide, 1 kg (1000 g) equals 2·2 lb or about 2 lb 3 oz. This method of conversion gives good results in nearly all cases, although in certain pastry and cake recipes a more accurate conversion is necessary to produce a balanced recipe.

Liquid measures

Imperial	Approx. millilitres to nearest whole figure	Recommended millilitres
¼ pint	142	150
½ pint	283	300
¾ pint	425	450
1 pint	567	600
1½ pints	851	900
1¾ pints	992	1000 (1 litre)

Oven temperatures

The table below gives recommended equivalents.

	°C	°F	Gas Mark
Very cool	110	225	¼
	120	250	½
Cool	140	275	1
	150	300	2
Moderate	160	325	3
	180	350	4
Moderately hot	190	375	5
	200	400	6
Hot	220	425	7
	230	450	8
Very hot	240	475	9

Notes for American and Australian users

In America the 8-oz measuring cup is used. In Australia metric measures are now used in conjunction with the standard 250-ml measuring cup. The Imperial pint, used in Britain and Australia, is 20 fl oz, while the American pint is 16 fl oz. It is important to remember that the Australian tablespoon differs from both the British and American tablespoons. The British standard tablespoon, which has been used throughout this book, holds 17·7 ml, the American 14·2 ml, and the Australian 20 ml. A teaspoon holds approximately 5 ml in all three countries.

Party Drinks

measuring guide

Still wines: Allow ½ bottle a head or an average of 6 glasses to a bottle.

Champagne and other sparkling wines: Calculate on 6 champagne glasses to a bottle, or allow ⅓ bottle per person for large numbers, or 1 bottle for 4 persons at a smaller party.

Spirits: 16 - 32 measures depending on size of measure with 1 fluid oz. (or a liqueur glass) being an average domestic 'double' (bars normally reckon 24 - 32 measures per bottle).

Sherry: 12 - 15 glasses a bottle. Allow an average of 1½ glasses per person with other drinks, or a bottle among 6 people at a 'sherry only' party.

Wine cups: Allow ¾ - 1 pint per person.

Liqueurs: Allow 1 to 1½ fluid oz. or 1 liqueur glass per person.

Soft drinks: 1 pint a head or, to use with spirits, 2 splits, or about ½ pint a head.

Choosing wines

The following list is a rough guide, but it should not be taken as laying down any hard and fast rules.

Before the meal: French vermouth (plain or with gin), dry sherry or dry champagne.

With hors-d'oeuvre: Graves, Moselle, Pouilly-Fuissé, Tavel Rosé.

With soup: Pale dry sherry or dry Madeira.

With fish: Hock, dry champagne, white burgundy.

With chicken, turkey or veal: As for fish.

With mutton, lamb, beef, pork, duck, goose, game, venison, hare: Beaujolais, burgundy or other red wines.

With sweets: Sauternes, champagne.

With cheese and dessert: Port, brown sherry and Madeira.

With coffee: Brandy or liqueurs.

For a less formal dinner party, one wine may be served throughout the meal. If the main dish is fish or poultry, a dry or medium-sweet white wine might be chosen, such as dry champagne, graves, chablis or hock. If meat or game is the main course, choose a good beaujolais, burgundy or other red wine.

If you decide to serve two wines, one with the meat course and another for the sweet, remember to serve the dry wine first. Your wine merchant will usually prove most knowledgeable and helpful if you ask his advice. (Some wine merchants will let you return any unopened bottles of wine).

A jug of iced water and soft drinks should also be set on a side table for guests who do not take wine.

Fruit cup

you will need:

2 large bottles cider	sliced orange, lemon, and
1 large bottle tonic water	leaves of mint in season
1 can orange or grapefruit juice	ice cubes

1 Slice fruit into bowl.
2 Add fruit juice, tonic water and cider.
3 Add mint leaves and ice cubes.
4 Leave in the refrigerator or a cool place for one hour before serving.

White wine cup

you will need:

2 bottles white wine (chablis, white Bordeaux)	1 miniature bottle maraschino or cointreau
1 large bottle tonic water	sliced orange and lemon
1 bottle lemonade (split size)	sliced cucumber (optional)
	ice cubes

1 Slice fruit and cucumber (if used), into a large bowl or jug.
2 Add wine, tonic water, lemonade and maraschino or cointreau.
3 Leave in a refrigerator or cool place for an hour.
4 Add ice cubes and serve.

Sangria

you will need:

2 bottles red wine (Spanish burgundy for preference)	sliced apples, oranges, lemons and peaches (in season)
2 large bottles soda water	ice cubes

1 Prepare the sangria about an hour before serving. Slice fruit into a large jug.
2 Add wine and soda water.
3 Leave in the refrigerator or in a cool place for at least one hour.
4 Add ice cubes and serve.

Mint julep

you will need:

3 pints ginger ale	mint leaves, pineapple
½ pint lemon squash	cubes and cocktail
½ pint water	sticks (optional)

1 Wash the mint leaves, pull off the stems and place in a bowl.
2 Add lemon squash and water; leave in a cold place for at least 30 minutes.
3 Add ginger ale, chilled if possible, pour into glasses and serve at once.
4 If liked, garnish with a pineapple cube on a cocktail stick.

For a real party touch, frost the glasses: Put the white of an egg into a saucer, fill another saucer with castor sugar. Dip the rim of each glass in the egg white then into the sugar. Leave in a cool place until dry.

Cider cup for 24 people

you will need:

4 pints water	1 bottle lemon squash
8 pints cider	2 small bottles ginger ale
1 bottle orange squash	

1 Add the water to the cider, then add orange and lemon squash.
2 Chill, and just before serving, add the ginger ale.

Fruit punch (non-alcoholic, serves 50)

you will need:

1 lb. sugar	1 pint pineapple juice
½ pint water	6 pints iced water
½ pint strong tea (freshly made)	½ bottle maraschino cherries
1 pint fruit syrup	1 large bottle soda water
½ pint lemon juice	mint, orange, lemon and apple for garnishing
1 pint orange juice	

1 Boil sugar and ½ pint water for 5 minutes.
2 Add the tea, strained, fruit syrup and juices. Leave in a cold place.
3 When required, add iced water and soda water, pour into a punch bowl.
4 Garnish with slices of fresh fruit and mint. Slices of red skinned eating apple look attractive in a punch, but to prevent discolouration, brush the slices with some of the lemon juice.

Hot punches

Ale punch

Mix together in a saucepan 2 pints of mild ale, 1 wineglass sherry, 1 wineglass brandy, 4 tablespoons sugar, rind and juice of 1 lemon and a pinch of grated nutmeg. Bring to the boil, strain and serve at once.

Cider punch

Mix together in a saucepan ½ pint sugar syrup (made with 4 oz. sugar and ½ pint water), 1 quart cider – draught if possible, 2 sliced oranges, 1 sliced lemon, and 1 teaspoon ginger. Bring to the boil and serve.

Rum punch

Put 3 pints cold water and 1 lb. lump sugar into a saucepan. Add the thinly peeled rind of ½ lemon and 1 orange. Stir until the sugar is dissolved, then bring to the boil and simmer for 5 minutes. Remove the pan from the heat and add the juice of 1 lemon and 4 oranges, and ½ pint strong tea. Strain, add ¾ - 1 pint rum and serve at once.

Hot wine punch

Put ½ pint water and 2 oz. sugar into a saucepan and stir until the sugar is dissolved. Add 1 pint red wine, a little lemon rind and a stick of cinnamon. Bring to the boil and boil for 1 minute. Add ¼ pint rum, strain and serve.

Claret cup

Mix together in a saucepan 3 lumps of sugar, 1 slice of lemon, ½ pint claret, and a small stick of cinnamon. Bring to the boil, strain and serve at once.

Party drinks made with coffee

Hot

Americano

Top cups of piping hot black coffee with swirls of sweetened whipped cream and sprinkle each with powdered chocolate.

Coffee whisk

Dissolve 2 heaped teaspoons instant coffee in 1 tablespoon boiling water. Beat in 1 small egg yolk. Whisk the white until stiff. Heat ½ pint milk and pour on to the coffee. Divide the egg white between 2 mugs or large cups and pour on the hot coffee. Serve at once.

Java mocha

Mix equal quantities of hot black coffee with hot milky chocolate or cocoa. Sweeten to taste. Pour into cups and float a marshmallow on each.

Chinatown

Mix 1 level teaspoon ground ginger into 1 pint black coffee. Pour into cups and serve topped with a little cream and a sprinkling of ground nutmeg or cinnamon.

Cold

Coffee flip

Whisk ½ pint cold white coffee, sweetened to taste, with 1 egg. Pour into glasses and sprinkle with a little ground nutmeg. If liked, a dessertspoon of rum or brandy may be whisked in with the egg and coffee.

Coffee coolie

Pour chilled black coffee into glasses and top with spoonfuls of vanilla or coffee flavoured ice cream and a little whipped cream.

Iced Coffee

you will need:

½ pint milk	vanilla essence
6 oz. castor sugar	½ pint cream
2 pints strong black coffee, hot	

1 Put the milk and sugar into a saucepan and bring almost to the boil. Add the coffee and a few drops of vanilla essence.
2 Allow to cool and strain.
3 Stir in the cream and chill until it has the consistency of thick cream.
4 Serve very cold, in tall glasses. Serve castor sugar separately.

Cheese and Wine Parties

This is one party that remains popular, year after year, because it is so easy to prepare and such fun for everyone—whether for an informal gathering of friends or for a special occasion. The menu is simple and allows the hostess plenty of scope to add her own personal touch—a good selection of cheeses, red and white wines, bread and butter are the essentials. To add colour and interest to the table, include relishes, pickles and fresh fruit. Apple pie or a rich fruit cake are delicious with cheese and can be served as a sweet course. If you prefer, serve a gâteau and coffee to finish the meal.

Quantities
Allow 1 lb. of cheese for every 4 guests. English country cheeses are excellent for this type of party, and the following give a well-balanced selection:

> Leicester
> Caerphilly
> Wensleydale
> Blue Stilton
> Sage Derby
> Cheshire
> Cheddar

If you prefer to add a continental touch to the cheese board, replace some of the English cheeses with two or three of the following:

> Camembert
> Brie
> Port Salut
> Gorgonzola
> Bel Paese
> Edam
> Emmental
> Samsoe
> Danish Blue

The wine
Allow ½ bottle of wine per person; most people prefer red wines with the stronger cheeses, and lighter wines, white or rosé, with the milder and softer cheeses. You might include some sherry, Madeira or port, if the budget allows, to complement the other wines you are serving. Choose your wines from the following list:

With mild cheeses
Yugoslav Riesling, German Rhine and Moselle wines, white Burgundy, white Bordeaux, dry white Spanish wines.

With mellow cheeses
Tavel Rosé, Anjou Rosé, red Bordeaux, Portuguese red wine, Australian claret-type wine.

With strong cheeses
Red Burgundy, red Rhône wine, Straccali Chianti, Hungarian Bull's Blood, and fortified wines: port, sherry, Madeira.

Allow plenty of bread and make the choice as varied as possible; for example, Vienna, French, rye or pumpernickel, and include some biscuits to give variety of texture—crispbread and wholemeal biscuits are good. Allow 1 lb. butter for 15 people (1 lb. butter makes 40 pats) and include some French, Danish and Scottish butter in the selection; your guests will find the different flavours interesting.

Preparation
A short time before the party, put the cheeses out on large plates. The cheeses may be left whole and garnished with fruit, small bunches of grapes, or sections of oranges and apples (do not forget to brush the cut surface with lemon juice to prevent discolouring). Alternatively, cut the cheese into cubes or fingers and label each plateful so that your guests can easily recognise which cheese they are eating.

Soft cheeses are best served whole, and rounds of cream cheese can be gárnished with mandarin oranges or maraschino cherries to give a party look.

For colourful and tasty extras, arrange small dishes of radishes, pickled walnuts, gherkins and tiny pickled onions—with cocktail sticks nearby. For an unusual touch, serve small bowls of nuts and raisins. Watercress and celery will add colour too, and are good accompaniments to most cheeses. See that the different kinds of bread and butter are well distributed so that everyone can easily help themselves. Have plates, knives and napkins at either end of the table, or on a separate table within easy reach. It is always a good idea, too, to serve the wine at a small table or from a trolley or sideboard away from the food, so that there is less danger of spilling.

Serving the wine
All red wine should be served at room temperature and opened at least one hour before drinking. All rosé and white wines should be

chilled for at least three-quarters of an hour before drinking, but do not keep wine in the refrigerator longer.

Glasses

Tulip-shaped goblets which hold 5 - 6 oz. are suitable for any wine. Glasses can be hired from most wine merchants free of charge provided that you buy your wine from them. They will charge for breakages. Ask to be supplied with Paris goblets, 5 - 6 oz. size.

Hallowe'en Party

The colours associated with this festival are red, orange and black, and the general effect should be one of spookiness. Black and orange paper streamers can be hung across the room with hanging lanterns. To decorate the walls, hang masks, or make large silhouettes of cats, bats, etc., cut from black or orange paper. Make a background of silver foil to represent moon-beams and add red or sequin eyes for glitter. Or drape the walls with realistic witches made from coat-hangers, with masks fastened to the hooks, black material draped over the hangers and white gloves pinned to the sleeves for the eerie effect. The table might be covered with small broomsticks, witches' caps, and black cats cut out in black paper, with candles in holders made of orange skins (cut oranges in half, scoop out the flesh—this can be used in a fruit salad—and dry the skins out in a cool oven). There are also the traditional Jack o' Lanterns made of pumpkin, turnip or swede. Autumn fruits, vegetables and nuts can also be used to set the scene, and anything associated with black magic.

The food :

Carry out the colour scheme where possible; for example, you might serve pizza, decorated with sliced black olives and tomatoes.

Other suggestions are:

A large platter of salad consisting of grated carrots, stuffed tomatoes, sliced red peppers, dessert apples, black olives and pickled walnuts and cubes of orange coloured Cheshire cheese.

Open sandwiches on rye or pumpernickel bread.

Orange jelly or cream, decorated with black grapes and mandarin oranges. Devils' Food Cake. Pumpkin Pie. Blackcurrant or Treacle Tart. Battenburg Cake made with chocolate and orange flavoured sponge. Do not forget chestnuts for roasting. Popcorn and toffee apples will be popular with young folk, too, also marshmallows, which can be toasted or stirred into mugs of hot cocoa, chocolate or black coffee.

Pizza

cooking time approximately 20 minutes

you will need:

Dough:	Filling:
1 lb. flour	1 lb. strong Cheddar
2 level teaspoons salt	cheese
1 tablespoon oil	1 lb. fresh or canned
¼ pint water	tomatoes
½ oz. fresh yeast	pepper and sugar
1 teaspoon sugar	1 teaspoon basil or thyme
	anchovy fillets
	black olives
	additional oil for brushing
	dough

1 Mix flour and salt in a basin.
2 Dissolve the yeast and sugar in ¼ pint of the water.
3 Add the yeast liquid, oil and the remaining water to the dry ingredients, and mix to a soft dough.
4 Knead the dough on a lightly floured surface until smooth and elastic, about 5 minutes.
5 Shape the dough into a ball and leave to rise until double in size.
6 Knead the dough lightly again, and roll out into a long strip.
7 Brush the dough with oil, roll up like a Swiss roll. Repeat three times.
8 Divide the dough into six pieces, form each into a ball and roll out into a 6-inch circle.
9 Place the rounds on a greased baking tray and brush each with oil.
10 Grate the cheese. Slice fresh tomatoes, sprinkle with a little pepper and sugar, or drain canned tomatoes and season with a little pepper.
11 Cover each round of dough with alternative layers of cheese and tomatoes, finishing with a layer of cheese. Sprinkle with basil or thyme, decorate with anchovy fillets and olives.
12 Bake at the top of a very hot oven (450° F.—Mark 8) for 15 - 20 minutes. Serve hot or cold. One large pizza can be made from this mixture, roll out dough to fit a tin 12 by 16 inches, bake for about 30 minutes.

Orange cream

you will need:

1 orange jelly	½ pint thick pouring
¼ pint orange juice and water, mixed	custard
	¼ pint double cream

1 Dissolve the jelly in the juice and water. Leave to cool.
2 Stir the custard (which should be cool) into the jelly.
3 Whisk the cream and fold lightly into the mixture.
4 Pour into a glass bowl and leave to set.

Battenburg cake

cooking time 25 minutes

you will need:

8 oz. butter or margarine	milk if necessary
8 oz. sugar	orange colouring
3 eggs	½ oz. cocoa
8 oz. flour	8 oz. almond paste
1 teaspoon baking powder	apricot jam
vanilla essence	castor sugar

1 Grease and line two oblong tins.
2 Sieve flour and baking powder.
3 Cream fat and sugar, add 3 - 4 drops vanilla essence, beat in the eggs.
4 Fold in the flour, using a little milk if necessary to make a soft mixture.
5 Add a few drops of orange colouring to *half* the mixture, and spread into one tin.
6 Stir cocoa into the remaining mixture, using more milk if necessary.
7 Spread this mixture into the second tin.
8 Bake in a moderately hot oven (375° F.—Mark 5).
9 Turn out on to a wire tray and leave until cold.
10 Trim cakes to an equal size and cut each in two lengthways.
11 Spread sides with jam (warmed if too stiff to spread) and stick pieces together, alternating the colours. Press firmly into shape.
12 Roll almond paste into an oblong on a sugared surface.
13 Place cake on almond paste, making sure that all outside surfaces are spread with jam.
14 Press two edges of almond paste together, brushing edges with egg white, if necessary, to seal. Turn cake over so that the join does not show.
15 Crimp top edges of almond paste lightly, score the top with a sharp knife in lines, squares or diamonds.
16 Dust with castor sugar. Wrap tightly in foil or greaseproof paper and leave in a cool place for 2 - 3 days before cutting.

Devils' food cake

cooking time 30 minutes

you will need:

8 oz. self-raising flour	2 level tablespoons golden
2 level tablespoons cocoa	syrup
½ level teaspoon nutmeg	3 eggs
½ level teaspoon mixed spice	3 oz. sultanas
1 level teaspoon cinnamon	½ level teaspoon vanilla essence
6 oz. butter or margarine	4 tablespoons milk
5 oz. castor sugar	

1 Grease two 8-inch sandwich tins.
2 Sieve together the flour, cocoa and spices.
3 Cream the fat and sugar until light and fluffy and add the essence.
4 Beat in the syrup (warmed, if liked) and the eggs.
5 Fold in the flour, adding milk to make a soft mixture.
6 Divide between the two tins. Bake at 375° F. —Mark 5.
7 Turn on to a wire tray and leave until cold.
8 Sandwich together and coat with frosting. Sprinkle thickly with coarsely grated plain chocolate.

Frosting

you will need:

10 oz. icing sugar	3 drops each vanilla and
5 oz. butter	almond essence
	1 dessertspoon milk

1 Sieve the icing sugar.
2 Beat the butter until soft, beat in sugar and essence and continue beating until very light and fluffy.
3 Beat in the milk.

Pumpkin Pie

cooking time about 45 minutes

you will need:

½ pint cooked, sieved pumpkin	2 tablespoons brandy
	about ¼ pint milk
¼ teaspoon each ground ginger and nutmeg	4 oz. castor sugar (approximately)
pinch of cinnamon	8 oz. shortcrust pastry
3 eggs	

1 Line a 9-inch pie plate with some of the pastry.
2 Mix the pumpkin, spices, beaten eggs, brandy and sufficient milk to give a thick batter consistency. Sweeten to taste.
3 Pour the mixture into the pastry lined plate and cover with pastry.
4 Bake in a moderately hot oven (375° F.—Mark 5) until cooked. Serve hot.

Toffee apples

you will need:

1 lb. sugar
4 oz. butter

2 tablespoons water
12 apples

1 Wash the apples and put a clean stick into each so that it feels firm.

2 Put all the ingredients for the toffee into a strong saucepan and allow the sugar to dissolve very slowly over a low heat.

3 Boil to the 'small crack' degree (290° F.). Dip each apple into cold water, then into the toffee, and then into cold water. Put on oiled slab to set.

The Perfect Party

So often one hesitates to give a party, feeling unable to cope with the problem of preparing the food and acting as a hostess at the same time. But anyone who has visited Denmark will know that it is possible to give a wonderful party based on their famous open sandwiches or 'smørrebrød'.

This is an ideal party for any occasion and everything can be prepared beforehand. You will find that this is one party that you can give with complete confidence—nothing can go wrong at the last minute. But as with all parties, the secret is careful organisation, which leaves the hostess unflurried and calmly waiting for the first guest. Work out a shopping list, and allow a period of preparation for washing salads and cooking and cooling some of the trimmings, like the scrambled eggs and the bacon. Let the butter get warm so that it is just right for spreading. Then you will be ready for the final stage in a calm frame of mind.

Allow 3 smørrebrød for each guest, and serve cheese, accompanied by rye bread or crispbread, or use it as a sandwich topping. Fruit, Danish pastries or a gâteau, and coffee, complete the menu; lager and aquavit are the natural drinks to serve with the smørrebrød.

Serve the smørrebrød on trays covered with foil.

The filled trays can be decorated with a little extra lettuce leaves, radish roses or tomato baskets. Smørrebrød can be prepared several hours in advance and left covered with a slightly dampened cloth in a cool place until needed.

Start your guests off with the fish sandwiches, then serve the meaty kinds and finally serve cheese. Be prepared to provide your guests with knives and forks for the smørrebrød.

When making the sandwiches

prepare sufficient pieces of well buttered rye or white bread to allow one piece for each sandwich required. Arrange all the 'topping' or filling so that every piece of the bread is covered.

Suggested toppings

Pickled herring and lemon

Can pickled herring or fillet of herring in tomato sauce
Lemon
Lettuce

Place lettuce leaf on each piece of bread. Top with fillet of herring. Complete with lemon twist.

Egg and caviare

Hard-boiled egg, sliced
Jar Danish caviare
Mayonnaise
Parsley

Arrange up to 6 slices of egg on each piece of bread. Pipe a little mayonnaise on the centre of each. Press 1 teaspoon Danish caviare on top of mayonnaise. Garnish with parsley sprig (sliced tomato and a sprinkling of chopped chive with egg is also very popular).

Liver pâté and bacon

1 can liver pâté
Crisp fried streaky bacon rashers
Fried, sliced mushrooms
Cucumber slices or cooked beetroot

Spread liver pâté thickly on buttered bread. Place bacon rasher on each. Spoon a few mushroom slices around bacon. Top with cucumber or beetroot twist. (Drain beetroot).

Tongue and Russian salad

Sliced tongue, thinly cut
Russian salad
Tomatoes
Cucumber slices

Arrange 3 small slices of tongue on each piece of bread. Fold slices, pressing them lightly into the butter to give a little height. Top with dessertspoonful Russian salad. Finish with tomato and cucumber twists.

Salami and onion rings

Salami slices
Onion
Parsley

Allow 3 slices of salami for each piece. Fold the slices and press lightly on to the butter. Garnish with 3 - 4 raw onion rings and a little parsley. Add a strip of meat jelly if liked.

Pork luncheon meat

1 can pork luncheon meat
5 fl. oz. double cream ⎫ mixed
Horseradish sauce ⎭
Orange
Prunes, cooked and stoned

Place 3 thin slices of meat on each piece of buttered bread. Top with horseradish cream (see below). Garnish with an orange twist (complete with peel) and place half prune on either side for contrast.

Horseradish cream

Whip the double cream until stiff, then mix with 2 tablespoons ready-made horseradish sauce.

Bacon and apple

Apple sauce (see below)
Streaky bacon rashers
Lettuce

Place lettuce leaf on each piece of bread. Place two tablespoons of apple sauce on top and garnish with rasher of bacon.

Apple sauce

Cut the cored apples into pieces and cook gently in bacon fat. Do *not* add water. When soft, sweeten very sparingly. The bacon fat gives the sauce a slight bacon flavour to blend with the rashers on top.

Ham and scrambled egg

Sliced, cooked ham
Scrambled eggs
Tomato
Cress

Place piece of ham on each piece of bread to cover completely. Place strip of egg diagonally across. Garnish with two small snippets of tomato and a little cress.

Danish blue

Danish blue cheese
Black grapes

Cut Danish blue into slices, or crumble and spread thickly on buttered bread. Top each slice with two halves of de-seeded black grapes. Walnuts or sliced stuffed olives may be used.

Samsoe cheese

Samsoe cheese
Bunch of radishes

Cut cheese into thin slices and place on top of buttered bread so that all the edges are covered. Garnish with radish rose.

Ingredients needed to make smørrebrød for twelve

36 pieces of rye and/or white bread approximately 2 by 4 inches.
8 oz. butter
6 oz. Samsoe cheese
6 oz. Danish blue cheese
4 eggs
4 oz. can liver pâté
6 oz. tongue (12 slices)
12 oz. salami (12 slices)
17 oz. can pork luncheon meat
4 oz. streaky bacon (7 rashers)
1¾ oz. jar Danish caviare
6 oz. pickled herring or fillet of herring in tomato sauce
4 oz. sliced ham
bottle horseradish sauce
6 oz. can cream
4 oz. mayonnaise
4 oz. Russian salad
4 oz. cooking apples
3 oz. mushrooms
1 small onion
1 orange
1 lemon
bunch radishes
2 oz. black grapes
¾ cucumber
1 lettuce
2 tomatoes
3 cooked stoned prunes
8 oz. cooked beetroot
little meat jelly if liked
little parsley, chives, and/or cress—these are usually interchangeable.

Danish meringue gâteau

cooking time about 4 hours

you will need:

Meringue:

4 egg whites	8 oz. sugar

Custard filling:

1 pint milk	2 eggs, plus 2 yolks
4 oz. sugar	1 vanilla pod
4 oz. flour	

Decorating:

1 lb. prunes (cooked)	½ pint double cream

1 Prepare meringue mixture (see page 31).
2 Pipe a ring of meringue 8 inches in diameter on to a baking tray which has been brushed lightly with oil. Use a large star pipe for this, and pipe a single small meringue on to the baking sheet also.
3 Pipe a complete round of meringue, about 1 inch larger than the ring on to another baking sheet.
4 Bake at 240° F.—Mark ¼ until firm and crisp, about 4 hours. Leave until cold.
5 Make custard, blend eggs, sugar and flour until creamy.
6 Heat milk with the vanilla pod until almost boiling, remove pod.
7 Pour milk on to the blended mixture, stirring throughout.
8 Return mixture to pan, and bring slowly to boiling point, stirring. Remove from heat and leave until cold.
9 Whisk cream until stiff.
10 To serve, place the round base of meringue on to a serving dish, cover with a layer of custard filling and a layer of prunes. Place the ring of meringue on top, using a little of the cream if necessary to hold it in position. Fill centre of ring with custard and prunes.
11 Decorate gâteau with piped cream and remaining prunes, placing small meringue on top.
Provided they have been dried out completely, the meringue layers may be made several days before they are required. The custard and prunes may be cooked the day before.
To cook the prunes, soak overnight, simmer in just enough water to cover, until tender. A little sugar and lemon rind may be added to the water. Drain well.

Danish pastry

cooking time 12 - 15 minutes

you will need:

8 oz. plain flour	1 oz. lard (white fat)
pinch salt	1 level tablespoon castor sugar
1 egg	
4 tablespoons cold water	½ oz. yeast, creamed with 1 tablespoon water
5 oz. Danish butter	

1 Sieve flour and salt into a bowl and rub in the lard.
2 Add the egg, sugar and water to the creamed yeast.
3 Pour into the flour mixture and mix to a soft dough.
4 Turn the dough out of the bowl and knead lightly until smooth.
5 Cover and allow to rest in a cool place for 10 minutes.
6 Beat the butter until soft and shape into an oblong block about ½ inch thick.
7 Roll the dough into a square, slightly larger than the butter.
8 Place the butter in the centre of the dough. Fold the sides of the dough over the butter so that they overlap down the centre. Seal in the butter by pressing lightly with the rolling pin.
9 Roll dough into an oblong strip about three times as long as it is wide. Fold evenly in three, cover and leave for 10 minutes.
10 Repeat rolling and folding twice more. Cover and leave to rest for a further 10 minutes in a cool place. Roll out and use as required.

Butter horns

1 Make dough as above and cut in half.
2 Roll one piece of dough into a circle about 9 inches across.
3 Trim to a good shape if necessary.
4 Divide circles into eight sections. Cut a small slit lengthways near the pointed end of each section. Place a small piece of almond paste in the middle of the short side of each.
5 Roll up each section from the short side to the point and curl into a crescent shape.
6 Place on a greased baking sheet about 1 inch apart. Brush with beaten egg.
7 Leave in a slightly warm place to prove for 15 - 20 minutes.
8 Bake in a hot oven (425° F.—Mark 7).
9 Brush with glacé icing while still warm and sprinkle with flaked blanched almonds.
10 Roll out second piece of dough and finish in the same way. Each piece makes eight horns.

Imperial stars

1 Make basic Danish pastry dough and cut in half.
2 Roll out dough into a rectangle 12 by 6 inches and cut into eight 3-inch squares.
3 Place a small piece of almond paste in the centre of each square.
4 Make a diagonal slit from each corner, half way to the centre of each square.

5 Fold the right-hand point of the sections to the centre of each square. Press firmly into position and brush with beaten egg.

6 Place on a greased baking sheet, leave to prove for 15 - 20 minutes.

7 Bake at 425° F.—Mark 7.

8 Pipe a swirl of confectioners custard into the centre of each or drop a teaspoonful of glacé icing into the centre and stud with half a glacé cherry. Finish the outer piece of dough in the same way.

Fruit whirls

1 Make basic Danish pastry dough and cut in half.

2 Roll one piece of dough into an oblong 12 by 8 inches.

3 Spread dough with spiced butter and sprinkle with a few sultanas and some finely chopped peel.

4 Cut strip of dough in half lengthways. Roll each piece up from the short end to make a fat roll about 4 inches wide. Cut into four 1-inch slices.

5 Place cut side down on a greased baking sheet and brush with egg.

6 Prove and bake as above.

7 To finish, coat with glacé icing and sprinkle with chopped almonds.

Spiced butter

Cream 2 oz. Danish butter with 2 oz. icing sugar and 2 level teaspoons cinnamon.

Confectioners custard

Blend 2 egg yolks, 1 oz. sugar and ½ oz. flour to a smooth paste. Stir in ¼ pint boiling milk. Return to the heat and stir until just boiling. Remove from the heat, add a few drops vanilla essence and leave until cold.

Almond paste

Blend 2 oz. ground almonds with 2 oz. castor sugar and enough egg white to make a stiff paste. Add 3 - 4 drops almond essence.

Buffet Supper

Much of the success of a buffet supper depends on the preparation of the table. The table should be as long as possible, with at least two serving points for each kind of food. Arrange plates, napkins and cutlery at either end of the table and try to have a small table or trolley available for serving drinks—and later for the coffee. Guests will be quite happy to help themselves, but it is a good idea to have one or two friends helping to see that things run smoothly. It is important to choose food that can be easily eaten with a fork. A hot rice dish is good for this kind of meal. Allow 2 oz. rice per person, cook it in plenty of boiling salted water, drain and keep it hot. Just before serving, add cubes of ham, chicken or roast beef, toasted almonds, sultanas, cubes of eating apple tossed in lemon juice and cooked peas. Serve with bowls of salad and small dishes of chutney, pickles and strips of pepper. Any of the following recipes are suitable for a buffet supper or a small supper party.

A supper party for a few guests can be quite an informal party. Serve small savouries with a drink as the first course. A pie or flan with salad, or a casserole dish to follow. If you are serving from a trolley or small table, make sure that you choose a dish which is 'manageable' with a fork. To finish the meal—cheese and fruit, or a dessert cake with coffee.

Savoury onion quiche

cooking time about 55 minutes

you will need:

Pastry:	4 oz. mushrooms, sliced
8 oz. plain flour	1 packet onion sauce mix
pinch salt	¼ pint milk
5 oz. butter	¼ pint single cream
Filling:	1 egg
2 oz. bacon	little grated cheese

1 Sieve the flour and salt into a bowl. Rub in the softened butter. Press the mixture into a ball and leave for 30 minutes.

2 Place the dough in an 8-inch pie plate and press out with the finger tips until the plate is completely lined.

3 Prick the bottom and sides well with a fork and bake for 10 minutes in a hot oven (400° F. —Mark 6).

4 Fry the bacon and crisp and then chop.

5 Fry the sliced mushrooms in the remaining fat and place in the bottom of the partly cooked pastry case, with the bacon.

6 Blend the onion sauce mix smoothly with the milk, cream and beaten egg. Pour over the bacon and mushrooms.

7 Sprinkle with grated cheese and bake at 350° F.—Mark 4—for about 45 minutes.

Spaghetti - party style

cooking time about 30 minutes

you will need:

1 large onion	1 lb. spaghetti
3 oz. dripping	4 oz. salami, cut into small
2 oz. streaky bacon	pieces
4 oz. peeled tomatoes	8 oz. cheese, grated
4 oz. mushrooms	4 oz. grilled mushrooms
2 oz. flour	for garnish
¾ pint stock	salt and pepper

1 Chop and fry the onion in the dripping.
2 Add the bacon, cut in small pieces, the sliced tomatoes and sliced mushrooms. Fry gently for about 5 minutes.
3 Add the flour and cook for a few minutes, then gradually stir in the stock. Simmer gently for 15 minutes.
4 Meanwhile, cook the spaghetti in fast boiling salted water.
5 Drain well and return to the pan.
6 Add the sauce, salami, and half the grated cheese to the spaghetti, season to taste and mix well.
7 Put into an ovenproof dish and sprinkle with the remaining cheese.
8 Brown under a hot grill and garnish with the grilled mushrooms.

Chicken pineapple flan

cooking time 15 - 20 minutes

you will need:

8-inch flan case made with 6 oz. shortcrust pastry	small packet frozen peas
4 oz. bacon rashers	6 oz. cold cooked chicken
small can pineapple cubes	½ pint white sauce
	salt and pepper

1 Remove rind from rashers, chop bacon and fry for about 5 minutes.
2 Drain pineapple, add to bacon and cook for a further 3 - 4 minutes.
3 Meanwhile cook peas and drain.
4 Chop chicken.
5 Heat sauce gently to boiling point, stirring all the time.
6 Add the bacon and chicken, half the pineapple and peas.
7 Season and pour into flan case.
8 Decorate with remaining pineapple and peas. Serves 6.

To save time at the last minute, both the sauce and flan case can be made the day before.

If the flan case has been cooked beforehand, heat it through on the middle shelf of a moderate oven for 15 minutes while the filling is being prepared. If the sauce has just been made, it is not necessary to reheat it.

Tuna flan

Make as for chicken pineapple flan, but use a 7 oz. can tuna, drained and flaked, in place of chicken and 1 chopped onion instead of pineapple. Decorate flan with anchovy fillets or sliced black olives and peas.

Lobster quiche

cooking time about 35 minutes

you will need:

1 8-inch flan case made with 6 oz. shortcrust pastry	4 oz. cooked lobster or 1 can lobster
2 eggs	1 oz. grated Parmesan cheese
½ pint double cream	seasoning

1 Bake the flan case 'blind' and allow to cool.
2 Flake the lobster into the pastry case.
3 Whisk the eggs, season to taste with salt and pepper and stir in the cream.
4 Pour over the lobster and sprinkle with grated cheese.
5 Bake in a moderate oven (350° F.—Mark 4) for 35 minutes until golden brown.

Creamy salmon pies

cooking time 30 - 35 minutes

you will need:

Pastry:	*Filling:*
8 oz. plain flour	1 10-oz. can condensed cream of celery soup
½ level teaspoon salt	or ½ pint thick white
1 level teaspoon caraway seeds (optional)	sauce
2 oz. each cooking fat and margarine	1 8-oz. can salmon
cold water	2 tablespoons chopped parsley
egg or milk for glazing	1 tablespoon lemon juice
celery salt	seasoning

1 Sift the flour and salt into a bowl and add the caraway seeds if used.
2 Rub the fats into the flour until the mixture is like breadcrumbs.
3 Mix to a stiff paste with cold water—about 3 - 4 tablespoons.
4 Turn on to a floured surface and roll out thinly. Cut out rounds of pastry with a biscuit cutter to line small patty tins. Cut slightly smaller rounds for tops and cut a small cross in the centre of each.
5 Flake the salmon, reserving its liquid.
6 Blend the soup or sauce, parsley, lemon juice and salt and pepper to taste and stir in the salmon and its liquid.
7 Fill the pastry lined patty tins with the salmon filling.
8 Dampen the edges with water and cover with pastry tops. Seal the edges and flake up with the back of a knife. Brush the tops with egg

or milk. Sprinkle each pie with a little celery salt.

9 Bake in a hot oven (400° F.—Mark 6) until pastry is cooked and brown.
10 Serve the pies hot or cold.

Savoury pie

cooking time 45 - 50 minutes

you will need:

6 oz. shortcrust pastry	3 large eggs, well beaten
1 medium sized onion, chopped	dash Worcestershire sauce
¼ pint milk	salt and pepper
2 oz. soft white breadcrumbs	bacon rolls
	watercress

1 Roll out the pastry and line an 8 - 9 inch pie plate.
2 Trim the edges and decorate.
3 Fry the onion until soft and golden brown and spread over the bottom of the pastry case.
4 Heat the milk, pour on to the breadcrumbs, then whisk in the eggs.
5 Add the Worcestershire sauce and salt and pepper to taste.
6 Stir well and pour the mixture into the prepared pie plate.
7 Bake in the centre of a moderately hot oven (375° F.—Mark 5).
8 When the pastry is golden brown and the custard set, remove from the oven and garnish with grilled bacon rolls and watercress.
9 Serve hot or cold with salad.

Chicken pilau

cooking time 25 - 30 minutes

you will need:

8 oz. cooked chicken	8 oz. Patna rice
2 tablespoons oil	2 tablespoons currants
1 onion, sliced	1¼ pints chicken stock
1 clove of garlic, crushed	1 level teaspoon salt
3 rashers streaky bacon, cut into strips	1 tablespoon chopped parsley
2 large tomatoes, peeled and chopped	1 lemon

1 Heat the oil in a large saucepan. Fry the onion, garlic, bacon and tomato gently for 5 minutes.
2 Add the unwashed rice and stir for 1 minute. Then add the currants and the chicken stock.
3 Bring to the boil and simmer uncovered for about 10 minutes. Add the chicken cut into strips and the salt and parsley.
4 Continue cooking for a further 10 - 15 minutes, stirring occasionally, until the rice is tender and all the liquid is absorbed.
5 Finally, stir in 1 tablespoon lemon juice, pile into a hot serving dish and garnish with lemon quarters.

Chicken and peach bake

cooking time 30 minutes

you will need:

2 packets potato crisps	3 oz. grated Cheddar cheese
1 lb. French beans or 1 large packet frozen beans	1 packet white sauce mix
	½ pint milk
8 oz. cooked chicken, sliced	1 1-lb. can sliced cling peaches
2 oz. sliced almonds	

1 Put three-quarters of the crisps over the bottom of a large casserole.
2 Arrange the cooked beans, chicken, almonds, and three-quarters of the cheese in layers on top of the crisps.
3 Make the sauce with the milk according to the directions on the packet. Pour over the ingredients in the casserole.
4 Arrange the remaining crisps round the edge of the casserole and bake in a moderate oven (350° F.—Mark 4) for 20 minutes.
5 Drain the peaches well. Remove the casserole from the oven and arrange the peaches over the top. Sprinkle with the remaining cheese and return to the oven for a further 10 minutes.

Hostess casserole

cooking time about 30 minutes

you will need:

1½ oz. butter	squeeze of lemon juice
1½ oz. plain flour	dash of Worcestershire sauce
¾ pint stock or milk	salt and pepper
1 lb. cooked turkey or chicken	*Topping:*
2 oz. cooked peas	4 slices bread
2 oz. cooked, chopped carrots	butter
	1 - 1½ oz. grated cheese

1 Melt the butter in a pan, add the flour and cook slowly for 1 minute.
2 Remove from the heat and gradually add the stock or milk. Reheat, stirring until the sauce comes to the boil and thickens.
3 Add the turkey or chicken, cut into small pieces, peas, carrots, lemon juice, Worcestershire sauce and salt and pepper to taste.
4 Cover the pan and heat through gently for 10 - 15 minutes.
5 Turn into an ovenproof dish.
6 Cut the crusts from the bread, spread the bread with butter, then cut each slice into four triangles.
7 Arrange triangles in an overlapping border round the edge of hot creamed mixture.
8 Sprinkle with cheese and brown under the grill or in a hot oven.
9 Serve with salad.

Virginia salad

you will need:

8 oz. cooked chicken or ham, diced	½ teaspoon salt
2 medium sized dessert apples	4 sticks celery, sliced
3 tablespoons lemon juice	1 tablespoon walnuts, chopped
3 tablespoons double cream	*Garnish:*
2 tablespoons salad cream	lettuce
	1 small red skinned apple
	sprigs of parsley

1 Peel and core the apples and cut into small dice.
2 Toss the apples in 1 tablespoon lemon juice.
3 Whip the cream lightly and blend into it the salad cream, salt and 1 tablespoon lemon juice.
4 Add the diced apple, chicken, celery and nuts. Mix together carefully and leave in a cool place.
5 To serve, arrange lettuce leaves on a flat dish and pile the chicken mixture in the centre.
6 Cut the unpeeled red skinned apple into slices, removing the core. Dip in the remaining lemon juice.
7 Garnish the salad with the apple and small sprigs of parsley.

Chicken and rice salad

you will need:

12 oz. cooked chicken	1 heaped tablespoon currants or raisins
8 oz. Patna rice, cooked	
1 clove of garlic, optional	1 green pepper
4 tablespoons salad oil	2 large tomatoes, skinned
salt and pepper to taste	1 - 2 tablespoons vinegar

1 Rub a salad bowl with the cut clove of garlic, if used.
2 Mix, in the salad bowl, the oil, vinegar (wine or tarragon if available) and the seasonings.
3 Add the hot rice and the currants or raisins and mix thoroughly.
4 Remove the seeds from the pepper and slice very finely.
5 Remove the seeds from the tomatoes and chop. Cut the chicken into small pieces.
6 Stir the chicken, pepper and tomato into the salad, reserving a few pieces of pepper and tomato for garnishing.
7 Cover and leave to stand for an hour before serving.
8 Sprinkle the remaining pepper and tomato over the salad before serving.

Spicy cheese cake

cooking time about 1 hour
you will need:

2 oz. plain tea biscuits	7 oz. castor sugar
2 level teaspoons castor sugar	grated rind of 1 lemon
¼ level teaspoon cinnamon	7 3-oz. packets cream cheese spread
¼ teaspoon (level) grated nutmeg	juice ½ lemon
Fillings:	5 fl. oz. double cream
5 eggs	black and green grapes

1 Well grease an 8-inch ring with a removable base.
2 Crush the biscuits very finely with a rolling pin. Mix with the sugar, cinnamon and nutmeg. Sprinkle this mixture over the base and the sides of the tin.
3 Secure band of aluminium foil round the outside of the tin letting it stand an inch above the rim. Place on a baking tray.
4 Place the cream cheese in a bowl and beat until smooth. Add the lemon juice and mix it in well.
5 Whisk the eggs and sugar together until thick. Add the lemon rind and whisk again.
6 Gradually add the whisked mixture to the creamed cheese.
7 Pour into the prepared tin and bake at 350° F.—Mark 4. Remove the foil. Return the cheese cake to the oven and cook for a few minutes longer until the cake shrinks away from the sides of the tin.
8 Remove from the oven and gently push the cake out of the ring by its base. Allow to cool.
9 Whip the cream until just thick and spread over the top of the cake.
10 Remove the seeds from the grapes and use to decorate the top of the cake.

Peach trifles

you will need:

6 slices Swiss roll	2 tablespoons raspberry jam
3 tablespoons sherry (optional)	glazing syrup
6 canned peach halves	½ pint double cream
	1 oz. blanched almonds

1 Place a slice of Swiss roll on each plate and sprinkle with sherry if used.
2 Place a little jam in the centre of each peach, place a peach, cut side down, on each slice of roll.
3 Pour a little syrup over each peach and leave to set.
4 Whisk cream and swirl on top of the peaches.
5 Cut the almonds into slivers and 'spike' into the peaches.
Serves 6.

Glazing syrup:

Blend 1 teaspoon of cornflour with 3 tablespoons of peach juice. Bring to the boil, boil for 3 minutes, add 2 - 3 drops of red colouring.

Pineapple trifles:

Make as above, using canned pineapple rings.

Orange chocolate pie

you will need:

6 oz. digestive biscuits	1 small can evaporated
1 oz. butter	milk
3 oz. plain chocolate,	2 teaspoons lemon juice
grated	double cream (optional)
¼ orange jelly	

1 Place the biscuits between two sheets of grease-proof paper or foil and crush them into fine crumbs with a rolling pin.
2 Heat the butter and 2 oz. of the chocolate in a bowl over a pan of hot water until melted.
3 Put the biscuit crumbs into a bowl, add the melted chocolate and butter and mix together well with a fork.
4 Line the bottom and sides of a buttered 8-inch pie plate or sandwich tin with this mixture, pressing firmly into position. Leave in a cool place until firm.
5 Meanwhile, dissolve the jelly in a little hot water and make up to ¼ pint with cold water. Leave in a cool place.
6 Whisk the evaporated milk with lemon juice until thick.
7 When the jelly is almost setting, add it to the milk, whisking all the time.
8 Pile the mixture into the prepared case and leave to set.
9 Decorate with the remaining chocolate and whipped cream if liked.

Tipsy cake

you will need:

1 sponge cake (see	1 pint custard (see
page 73)	page 46)
raspberry jam	blanched almonds
1 glass sherry or Madeira	angelica
	glacé cherries

1 Split the sponge cake and spread thickly with jam.
2 Sandwich together again and place in a dish.
3 Pour the wine over the cake and leave to soak for 1 hour.
4 Pour the custard over the cake and stick blanched almonds into it to resemble a porcupine. Decorate with cherries and angelica.

Fresh fruit salad

you will need:

1 pint water or fruit	juice 1 lemon
juice to each pound of	1 tablespoon brandy
fruit and	(optional)
3 oz. sugar	2 tablespoons sherry
fresh fruit as available	(optional)

1 Prepare the syrup by boiling the water or fruit juice and the sugar together until it is reduced to half the quantity.
2 Prepare the fruit according to its kind. Apples should be peeled, cored and sliced. If liked the skin of a red skinned apple can be left on for colour. Oranges should be skinned and all traces of pith removed. The quarters can be halved if liked.
3 Remove the skins and seeds from grapes, leaving a few black grapes unpeeled for colour.
4 Halve apricots and peaches, remove the skin and cut each half in two.
5 Pineapple should be cut into slices or cubes after peeling. Remove the stones from cherries and halve and stone plums.
6 Hull strawberries and raspberries carefully and slice peeled bananas thinly.
7 Place the prepared fruit into a bowl. Cover with syrup and flavour with lemon juice. Cover the bowl and leave to become cold.
8 Stir the brandy and sherry, if used, into the salad just before serving. Serve with whipped cream.

Jellied fruit flan

Fill a cooked pastry flan case (see page 69) with drained, canned fruit. Heat ¼ pint fruit juice in a small pan. Stir in 2 teaspoons powdered gelatine. Heat gently until the gelatine dissolves, add sugar to taste.
Leave in a cool place until just about to set. Spoon over the fruit and leave until completely set.

Pineapple and cherry gâteau

you will need:

1 8-inch round sponge	1 small fresh pineapple **or**
cake (see page 73)	1 small can pineapple
1 egg white	rings
2 oz. castor sugar	fresh or canned cherries
¼ pint double cream	

1 Whisk the egg white until stiff. Add half the castor sugar and whisk again until stiff. Fold in the remaining castor sugar.
2 Line a baking tray with greaseproof paper.
3 Pipe small meringues on to the tray and bake in a very slow oven until dry and crisp. Cool on a wire tray.
4 Whisk the cream until thick.
5 Cut the sponge through the centre and sandwich together again with some of the cream.
6 Spread the remaining cream round the sides and on top of the cake. Mark the top with a fork to give a swirling effect and then mark with a knife into 8 portions.
7 Press the meringues all round the sides.
8 If using fresh pineapple, peel and cut into 6 slices. If using canned, drain 6 rings well.
9 Place on top of the gâteau and decorate with cherries.

Lemon cake dessert

cooking time about 35 minutes

you will need:

4 oz. self-raising flour	4 eggs
½ oz. butter	4 oz. castor sugar
3 tablespoons hot water	about ¼ pint double cream
grated rind 1 lemon	fresh strawberries

1 Sift the flour 3 times.
2 Melt the butter in the hot water and add the lemon rind.
3 Separate the egg yolks from the whites. The eggs should be at room temperature.
4 Whisk the whites until stiff, gradually adding the sugar.
5 When the mixture is stiff enough to stand in peaks, add the yolks and whisk until creamy.
6 Very lightly fold in the flour with a metal spoon, then fold in the liquid.
7 Pour the mixture into a greased and lined cake tin, 7 inches square by 2½ inches deep.
8 Bake in a moderately hot oven (375° F.— Mark 5).
9 Turn out and allow to cool on a wire tray.
10 Serve, topped with whipped cream and sugared strawberries.

This dessert cake can also be cooked in two 8-inch greased sandwich tins. Cook at the same temperature for 20 - 25 minutes.

Teenage Party

For a teenage party, the keynote is informality and it is best to clear the room of as much furniture as possible, providing plenty of cushions. Be sure to have a record or cassette player, and nominate someone to be responsible for compiling a list of records and tapes and noting the names of those who will be providing them; you should also be sure to include plenty of music that is fun to sit and listen to, as well as good dance numbers. The food should be as simple as possible; food that can be eaten with the fingers is usually most popular, and if it can be available in the kitchen (so that the crowd can drift in and help themselves) so much the better. The food can be based on the following: Soup, French bread, crispy fried chicken, sausages or hot dogs, spaghetti, potato crisps, potatoes baked in their jackets, dips, crisps and savoury biscuits, wedges of cheese and plenty of fresh fruit. Gâteaux made from basic sponge recipes and finished with different fillings and frostings, or flans or individual fruit pies will cater for the sweet tooth. Choice of food will depend to a large extent on the amount of money available—it is often quite the thing for some of the girls to share the supplying of the food, one being responsible for the soup and bread, another for the hot dogs, etc.

For an 'on the spur of the moment' party or record session, keep food really simple and provide soup, hot dogs, hamburgers, or spaghetti, bread and cheese, coffee and doughnuts.

Food for Twelve Teenagers

Soup: Allow 4 large cans or 3 packets, prepare at least 30 minutes before the party. Make hot dips just before the party and keep hot for serving; if this is not possible, make up beforehand and heat gently in a bowl over hot water 30 minutes before required. Cut two 2-ft. French sticks into 2-inch chunks for each dip.

Hot dogs:

cooking time 20 - 30 minutes

you will need:

12 long, soft bread rolls	salt and pepper
1¼ lb. (12) pork sausages	fat for frying
1 lb. onions	tomato sauce

1 Star to prepare 30 minutes before required.

Place a serving dish and a small bowl in a warm place.
2 Fry sausages in a large pan, turning occasionally to brown evenly.
3 Slice onions finely, melt enough fat to cover the bottom of the pan, add onions, fry slowly, stirring occasionally, until golden and soft (about 20 minutes). Sprinkle with a little salt and pepper while frying.
4 Split and butter rolls thinly, place on a dish.
5 Place sausages in a hot dish, onions in a bowl. Let guests assemble their own hot dogs (have tomato sauce available for those who do not like onions). See that there are plenty of paper napkins handy.

Coffee for 12 full mugs

1 oz. instant coffee	2½ pints water
2½ pints milk	1 lb. demerara sugar

1 Put water on to boil, milk to heat.
2 Put the coffee into a large hot jug, pour on a little boiling water. Stir well, pour on remaining boiling water.
3 Pour milk into a hot jug, serve milk and sugar separately.

Hot cheese dip

Stir 8 oz. grated cheese into 1 pint hot white sauce (see page 59), adding ½ teaspoon dry mustard, and salt and pepper to taste.

Hot mushroom dip

Make up 2 packets mushroom soup, according to instructions on the packet, but using only 1½ pints of water. Bring to boil, reduce heat, and simmer for 5 minutes. Stir in a 6-oz. can evaporated milk, sprinkle with grated nutmeg, keep hot but do not allow to boil.

Drinks

Cider: Allow 6 bottles of medium sweet cider or 12 large bottles of coca-cola, or serve lemonade or ginger-beer shandy, again allowing 3 good-sized glasses per person. Whichever drink you decide upon, serve it chilled.

Beefburgers

Mince 1½ lb. topside steak with 1 thick slice white bread and 1 peeled, medium sized onion. Add a pinch of salt, pepper and dry mustard. Form into twelve flat cakes, top each with a dab of fat, and place in the grill pan. Put under a hot grill, allowing 5 minutes on each side. Sandwich between soft buttered baps, serve with made mustard, pickle or tomato sauce.

Crispy fried chicken

Sprinkle chicken joints with lemon juice, salt and pepper, dip in beaten egg and toss in crumbs made from crushed potato crisps. Shallow fry in melted butter until crisp and golden, 20 - 30 minutes. Place in a hot dish and leave in a warm oven, covered, until required.

Fruit flans (each will cut into 6)

you will need:

2 8-inch pastry or sponge flan cases	1 packet lemon jelly
1 8-oz. can mandarin oranges	2 6-oz. cans evaporated milk
1 8-oz. can pineapple pieces	2 teaspoons lemon juice
	1 bar milk chocolate flake

1 Drain the fruit, keeping the mandarin oranges and pineapple separate, but pour all the juice into a measuring jug.
2 Make the juice up to ½ pint with water if necessary, pour into a pan. Place the jelly in the fruit juice, heat gently and stir until the jelly is dissolved.
3 Leave until cold and just beginning to set.
4 Pour the milk into a large bowl, add the lemon juice and whisk until thick and stiff. The milk will whisk up more easily if chilled beforehand.
5 Stir in the jelly, gradually, whisking all the time until the milk and jelly are well mixed and light and fluffy.
6 Divide the mixture in two, stir the oranges into 1 portion, and the pineapple into the other. Fill each flan case with a mixture.
7 Crumble chocolate flake over each, and leave in a cool place until required.

Parties for the 20-plus Age Group

Spaghetti alla Bolognese

cooking time about 1¼ hours

you will need:

1 lb. spaghetti	1 bay leaf
2 tablespoons butter	4 tablespoons tomato purée
4 tablespoons olive oil	½ pint beef stock
4 oz. green bacon, finely chopped	¼ pint dry wine
1 onion, finely chopped	salt, pepper and grated nutmeg
2 carrots, finely chopped	4 tablespoons double cream
1 stick celery, finely chopped	freshly grated Parmesan cheese
8 oz. sirloin of beef, minced	butter
1 strip lemon peel	

1 Heat the butter and olive oil in a large thick bottomed pan.
2 Add the bacon, onion, carrots, and celery and sauté over a medium heat, stirring occasionally for a few minutes.
3 Add the beef and stir until evenly browned.
4 Add the lemon peel, bay leaf, tomato purée, stock, wine, salt, pepper and nutmeg to taste.
5 Cover the pan and simmer for 30 minutes, stirring occasionally.
6 Remove the lemon peel and bay leaf and simmer uncovered for a further 30 minutes until the sauce has thickened slightly.
7 Add the cream and simmer for 2 - 3 minutes.
8 Meanwhile cook the spaghetti in boiling salted water until just tender. Drain and dot with butter.
9 Serve with the Bolognese sauce and the cheese.

Steak and cheeseburgers

cooking time about 15 minutes

you will need:

12 oz. topside steak	about 1 oz. butter or
1 slice bread	bacon dripping
1 onion	6 thin slices Cheddar
black pepper	cheese
1 level teaspoon salt	6 bap rolls, split and
salad	buttered
	made mustard

1 Mince together the steak, bread and the peeled onion. Season with a sprinkling of pepper and the salt.
2 Form the mixture into 6 flat cakes. Place in the grill pan without the rack and dot with butter or bacon dripping.
3 Grill under a medium heat, allowing 5 - 7 minutes on each side and turning two or three times during cooking.
4 Spoon the drippings in the pan over the burgers.
5 Place a slice of cheese on the bottom half of each roll, dab with mustard to taste and top each with a hot burger.
6 Place the tops back on the rolls and serve with salad or pickles.

Kebabs

cooking time 8 - 10 minutes

you will need:

4 small tomatoes	8 small pieces cooked
8 small mushrooms	meat
4 rashers streaky bacon	1 can sweet corn
4 chipolata sausages	½ oz. butter
2 oz. butter	4 skewers approximately
	8 inches long

1 Cut the tomatoes in half, peel the mushrooms if necessary. Remove the rind from the bacon, cut each rasher in half and roll up making 8 bacon rolls. Prick the sausages, twist the centre of each and cut through making 8 small sausages.
2 Thread on to each skewer, alternately, tomato, mushrooms, bacon rolls, sausages and pieces of meat. Brush well with melted butter.
3 Cook under a hot grill turning the skewers at intervals so that all the ingredients are cooked evenly, brushing again with butter during cooking.
4 Meanwhile, heat the corn in a small pan, drain, add the ½ oz butter. Toss the corn and turn into a hot dish.
5 Place the skewers on the corn and serve at once. Cubes of luncheon meat and pineapple may also be used.

Ham and pineapple loaf

cooking time about 1 hour

you will need:

12 oz. minced ham	little paprika pepper
1 onion finely chopped	pinch grated nutmeg
1 egg, beaten	salt and pepper
1 oz. white breadcrumbs	1 small pineapple or
1 green pepper, finely	6 canned pineapple
chopped	rings, drained
2 oz. luxury margarine	

1 Place the ham, onion, egg, breadcrumbs, green pepper, paprika pepper, nutmeg, salt and pepper to taste and the melted margarine in a bowl and mix thoroughly together.
2 Grease a 1-lb. loaf tin.
3 If using fresh pineapple, peel and cut into 6 rings.
4 Place 2 rings on the bottom of the tin, stand one at each end of the tin and one at each side of the tin.
5 Press the ham mixture into the tin and smooth the top.
6 Bake on the middle shelf of a moderately hot oven (375° F.—Gas Mark 5). Turn out of the tin and serve hot or cold with French bread.

Seafood pie

cooking time 30 - 40 minutes

you will need:

1 chopped onion	1 7-oz. can tuna
1½ oz. flour	lemon juice
½ pint milk	6 oz. shortcrust pastry
1 10-oz. can condensed	(see page 68)
mushroom soup	salt and pepper

1 Line a pie plate with pastry.
2 Chop the onion and cook in boiling salted water until tender.
3 Blend the flour with a little milk taken from the ½ pint. When quite smooth, stir in the remaining milk.
4 Heat the soup, blending in the milk. Bring to the boil.
5 Drain and flake the tuna and add to the sauce with the cooked onion and a good squeeze of lemon juice.
6 Season and pour into the pastry-lined plate. Bake in a hot oven (400° F.—Mark 6) for 30 minutes.

Australian ham pie

cooking time 30 minutes

you will need:

12 oz. shortcrust pastry	1 beaten egg
(see page 68)	4 oz. seedless raisins
4 oz. grated cheese	6 - 8 oz. chopped ham
½ pint thin white sauce	beaten egg or milk for
salt and pepper	glazing

1 Line a 9-inch pie plate with half the pastry.
2 Stir the cheese into the sauce, season to taste and add the egg.
3 Fill the pie plate with alternate layers of seedless raisins and chopped ham.
4 Pour the cheese sauce over the raisins and ham.
5 Cover the pie with the remaining pastry and seal the edges.
6 Brush with beaten egg or milk and make 3 small cuts in the top of the pastry.
7 Bake in a hot oven (400° F.—Mark 6) for 30 minutes, until golden brown.

Highland swags

cooking time about 35 minutes

you will need:

1 lb. pork or beef sausage meat	black pepper
1 oz. breadcrumbs	6 large hard-boiled eggs (shelled)
2 level teaspoons made mustard	12 oz. shortcrust pastry (see page 68)
¼ level teaspoon salt	

1 Mix the sausage meat, breadcrumbs, mustard, salt and a sprinkling of black pepper.
2 Divide the mixture into 6 equal portions and mould each portion round an egg.
3 Roll out the pastry and cut into 6 equal sized oblongs.
4 Moisten the edges with water and stand a meat-covered egg in the centre of each.
5 Draw the corners of the pastry up to the middle and press together to seal, then flute.
6 Stand on a lightly greased baking tray and cook in a hot oven (400° F.—Mark 6).
7 Serve hot or cold.

Super sandwiches

cooking time about 30 minutes

you will need:

1 bap loaf	1 egg
butter	1 level teaspoon salt
Filling:	1 teaspoon Worcester-shire sauce
1 lb. lean minced beef	
2 oz. breadcrumbs	little butter or bacon fat

1 Mix the beef, breadcrumbs, beaten egg, salt and the Worcestershire sauce together and shape into a large hamburger about 1 inch larger than the round of the bap.
2 Dot the top of meat with a little butter or bacon fat and place in a sandwich tin.
3 Cook for 30 minutes in a moderate oven (350° F.—Mark 4) or grill slowly, allowing 10 - 15 minutes each side.
4 Split the bap loaf in half and spread with butter.
5 Sandwich together with the hamburger and crisp lettuce, cut into four and serve with tomatoes and pickled onions.

Devilled pâté sandwiches

you will need:

8 slices bread	¼ level teaspoon dry mustard
4 oz. liver pâté or pounded liver sausage	½ teaspoon Worcester-shire sauce
1 tablespoon finely chopped onion	2 rashers bacon, halved and grilled
1 tablespoon tomato ketchup	

1 Lightly toast the bread on one side.
2 Pound the liver pâté or liver sausage, onion, and seasonings together.
3 Spread this mixture over the toasted sides of 4 slices of the bread.
4 Top each with half a rasher of grilled bacon and then with the remaining bread, toasted side down.
5 Toast both remaining sides, garnish with watercress and serve at once.

Egg and mushroom specials

you will need:

8 slices bread	2 tablespoons mayonnaise or soured cream
4 hard-boiled eggs	
2 - 4 oz. cooked mushrooms or 1 small can	4 rashers bacon salad

1 Lightly toast the bread on one side.
2 Blend the finely chopped eggs and mushrooms with the mayonnaise or cream. Season to taste.
3 Warm the mixture and spread over the toasted sides of 4 slices of the bread. Top with the remaining bread, toasted side down.
4 Toast both sides, the last lightly, then cover with halved bacon rashers. Toast until the bacon is crisp. Serve with salad.

French bread pizzaburgers

cooking time about 10 minutes

you will need:

1 French loaf, about 15 inches long	1 level teaspoon salt
1 lb. minced steak	½ teaspoon oregano
1 tablespoon finely chopped onion	2 tablespoons tomato ketchup or purée
2 tablespoons grated cheese	2 or 3 tomatoes
	extra cheese or anchovy fillets

1 Cut the bread into slices, ½ - ¾ inch thick.
2 Blend the steak, onion, cheese and seasonings. Spread over the bread slices.
3 Grill slowly for about 7 minutes until the meat is cooked.
4 Top each with a slice of tomato and cook a few minutes longer.
5 Sprinkle a little grated cheese on to each or top with an anchovy fillet.
6 Serve open or sandwiched in pairs, with salad.

Barbecue bean sandwiches

cooking time about 20 minutes
you will need:

8 slices white bread	1 teaspoon made mustard
1 8-oz. can beans in	4 oz. streaky bacon rashers
tomato sauce	4 slices Cheddar cheese
1 tablespoon horseradish	paprika pepper
cream	salad greens

1 Grill the bacon until crisp and crumble into pieces.
2 Toast the bread on one side. Top 4 slices (on the toasted side) with the beans blended with horseradish, mustard and bacon.
3 Top with remaining bread, toasted side down.
4 Toast one side, turn sandwich over and top with cheese. Toast until cheese melts.
5 Sprinkle with paprika and serve at once with green salad.

Egg and sausageburgers

cooking time about 20 minutes
you will need:

8 oz. pork sausage meat	4 baps
2 oz. fat	salt and pepper
4 eggs	tomato sauce or chutney

1 Divide the sausage meat into 4 equal portions, shape into thin flat cakes, using lightly floured hands.
2 Fry in hot fat until golden brown on both sides, drain and keep hot.
3 Fry the eggs in the remaining fat in the pan, spooning the hot fat over the top of the eggs to cook the yolk thoroughly.
4 Cut the baps in half and toast the inside of each.
5 Spread the bottom half of each bap with a little sauce or chutney, top each with a round of sausage meat and an egg.
6 Season with salt and pepper, cover each with the top half of the bap. Serve at once.

Egg and sausage roll

cooking time about 1 hour
you will need:

8 oz. shortcrust pastry	4 hard-boiled eggs
(see page 68)	beaten egg or milk to
1 lb. pork sausage meat	glaze

1 Roll pastry out thinly into an oblong 11 by 9 inches.
2 Flatten the sausage meat with floured hands into a piece 11 by 4 inches.
3 Place the sausage meat on the pastry, and place the eggs in a line along the centre. Fold the sausage meat over the eggs.
4 Brush the edge of the pastry with water, fold the pastry over the sausage meat, and press the edges of pastry together to seal.
5 Place the roll on a baking tray, brush with

egg or milk. Make a diagonal cut in the pastry over each egg.
6 Bake in a hot oven (400° F.—Mark 6) on third shelf from top for 30 minutes.
7 Reduce to moderately hot (375° F.—Mark 5) for further 30 minutes. Serve hot or cold. Serves 6 - 8.

King size sausage roll

Omit eggs, and add 1 chopped onion fried in 1 oz. butter and a pinch of mixed herbs to sausage meat, then make as above.

Raspberry gâteau

you will need:

2 8-inch rounds sponge	½ pint double cream
or sandwich cake	thick white glacé icing,
8 oz. raspberries	lemon flavoured (see
2 oz. castor sugar	page 80)

1 Mash half the raspberries with the castor sugar.
2 Spread over one cake, top with cream, whisked until thick and cover with second round of cake.
3 Coat with thick glacé icing and decorate with remaining raspberries.
4 Serve as soon as the icing is set.

Mandarin gâteau

Make as above, using drained mandarin oranges in place of the raspberries and omitting the castor sugar. Sprinkle the icing with coarsely grated chocolate and decorate with mandarins.

Strawberry meringue gâteau

Make as above, using strawberries instead of raspberries, piling more whipped cream with the strawberries on top of the cake. Decorate with small whole meringues or pieces of meringue.

Mincemeat apple pie

cooking time 30 minutes
you will need:

12 oz. shortcrust pastry	2 oz. ground almonds
(see page 68)	½ oz. flour
2 - 3 tablespoons mincemeat	2 oz. butter
1 lb. cooking apples	2 oz. sugar
juice ½ lemon	1 egg

1 Cut off two-thirds of the dough, roll out, and use to line a deep 9-inch pie plate.
2 Spread mincemeat in the bottom of the pie case.
3 Peel, core and slice the apples, arrange them over the mincemeat and sprinkle them with lemon juice.
4 Cream the fat and sugar, beat in the egg with a tablespoon of the ground almonds.
5 Fold in the flour and remaining almonds.
6 Spread mixture over the apples.

7 Damp the edge of the pastry; roll out the remaining pastry into a round the same size as the top of the pie.

8 Place the lid in position, press the edges together and flute.

9 Bake on the middle shelf of a hot oven (400° F. —Mark 6).

10 Cover the pie with greaseproof paper when sufficiently brown. Serve hot or cold with cream or cheese.   Serves 8 - 12.

Barbecue Party

A barbecue party is a most informal type of party and, perhaps, this is why it is so very popular. Barbecues are rather like glorified picnics; forget all the rules and your cookery book, but prepare everything beforehand and let your guests cook their own food—you can settle down to have fun, watching them. Whether you are building your barbecue or have a ready made one, there are one or two things to organise before you start.

Consider where the wind is coming from when choosing a site for the fire; it is miserable trying to cook with smoke in your face.

Light the fire at least one hour before you want to start cooking and make sure that the charcoal is red hot before you start cooking. If possible, arrange the fire so that you have one end for keeping food hot when cooking has been completed.

See that you **have** enough charcoal for the evening—to **cook one** good meal for 15 people, you will need about 12 lb. charcoal.

Provide plenty of long skewers or sticks for cooking. Brushes for basting, and a pot of melted butter, fat or oil should be handy. Plenty of paper napkins or kitchen paper will be useful too, and 'barbecue' aprons made of checked cotton or paper would be a thoughtful touch, to protect best dresses.

A trestle table and benches set up in the garden would be useful. Everything that is needed: knives, forks, bread and seasoning, should be easily available. And do try to arrange for the party to continue even if the weather does not hold out. Be prepared to convert the garage into a 'cafe' at a moment's notice.

Menu

Choose from the following:

Chicken joints—Cook on the rack of the fire, turning all the time, brush frequently with sauce or melted butter—cooking time 45 - 50 minutes.

Chops and cutlets—Cook for 10 - 12 minutes on the rack over the fire, or held on a fork or skewer.

Steak—Cut thick slices into cubes or fingers, brush with fat or oil and cook for 8 - 10 minutes. Liver can be cooked in the same way, also gammon rashers; allow 20 minutes for these.

Kebabs can be left to cook by themselves while other food is being done. Cooking time will depend on the ingredients used. (See recipes.)

Potatoes should be scrubbed, brushed with butter or fat, pricked, and put in the hot ash at the end of the fire, or arranged along the edge of the cooking grill. Turn frequently during cooking.

Soup, casseroles of rice or pasta, or potato, may be prepared in the kitchen and carried out to the party and kept hot at the side of the fire. Salads, bread and cheese, and home-made pies complete the menu, and will ensure that everyone is well fed—and don't forget the drinks! 'Barbecuing' is thirsty work.

To ensure really delicious 'bites' prepare a marinade and allow the meat, already cubed or sliced to stand in this for several hours beforehand; alternatively, make a good barbecue sauce for brushing the meat with while it is being cooked.

Guide to quantities

$3\frac{1}{2}$ lb. chicken will serve 6 people.

Allow 8 oz. steak per person.

Serve 4 sausages per person if they are the main part of the meal, or 1 sausage per person if other things are provided.

For kebabs—allow about 8 oz. meat per person.

1 lb. potatoes will serve 4 people.

If you feel you just cannot cope with the hazards of a barbecue—hold a 'cook in'—an informal barbecue party in the 'security' of home. All these dishes can be cooked in the traditional way, and if you have a rôtisserie spit, you can try more elaborate dishes.

Building a Barbecue

A simple barbecue is made with house bricks and a metal grill. Build the walls with two layers of bricks, leaving open the end facing the wind, as shown in the sketch.

It is, of course, possible to make a much more elaborate barbecue with a brick wall, roof and paved area, too, so that guests can eat outside in comfort. If you require this kind, it will probably be necessary to employ a builder.

However, for a small party, the simple barbecue should be quite sufficient. Before building the barbecue cut and remove a piece of turf—that is if you are using it on a lawn—and replace it afterwards. The illustration also shows how a useful extension may be constructed to hold a covered pan in which to keep cooked food hot.

To get charcoal to glow, roll small balls of newspaper tightly together and arrange them among the charcoal. Set them alight and the charcoal should begin to burn. It burns for about two hours and can be left to burn out.

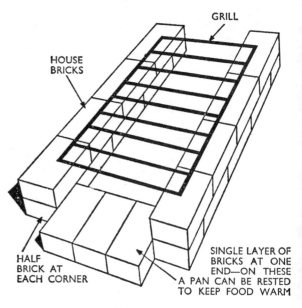

GRILL

HOUSE BRICKS

HALF BRICK AT EACH CORNER

SINGLE LAYER OF BRICKS AT ONE END—ON THESE A PAN CAN BE RESTED TO KEEP FOOD WARM

Steak and mushroom kebabs

cooking time about 20 minutes

you will need:

1 lb. steak	2 tablespoons tomato
12 small mushrooms	ketchup
¼ pint red wine	1 level teaspoon sugar
¼ pint corn oil	½ level teaspoon salt
1 teaspoon Worcestershire	1 tablespoon vinegar
sauce	pinch dried marjoram
1 clove garlic (chopped	pinch dried rosemary
finely)	

1 Cut the steak in small cubes and peel and stalk the mushrooms.
2 Mix all the other ingredients together in a basin and add the steak and the mushrooms.
3 Leave to marinate for 2 hours, then alternate steak squares and mushrooms on skewers and grill until tender, basting frequently with the marinade.

Lamb en brochette

cooking time about 20 minutes

you will need:

1-1½ lb. lean lamb	¼ teaspoon freshly
4 tablespoons corn oil	ground pepper
3 tablespoons soy sauce	1 onion, grated finely
	2 tablespoons lemon juice

1 Mix all the ingredients together to make a marinade.
2 Cut lamb into cubes and leave in the marinade for an hour or longer, turning frequently.
3 Thread on skewers and grill until tender.

Skewer tidbits

Button onions, apple slices, stuffed olives, gherkins, pineapple chunks, peach halves, prawns, pieces of banana wrapped in bacon rashers or ham. Baste vegetables and fruits with corn oil while grilling.

Baked potato sandwiches

cooking time about 1 hour

you will need for each person:

1 large old potato	1 thin slice cheese
1 back rasher bacon	seasoning
1 pat butter	

1 Scrub the potatoes and cook them in wood-fire embers.
2 Meanwhile cook the rashers slowly over the fire.
3 When the potatoes are cooked, split them lengthways and spread the butter.
4 Add the cheese and finally the bacon. Season to taste with salt and pepper.
5 Close the potato 'sandwich' and eat it hot.

Quick barbecue sauce

cooking time 5 - 10 minutes

you will need:

1 oz. butter or margarine	2 tablespoons vinegar
1 small onion, chopped	1 dessertspoon chutney
1 packet tomato soup	¼ pint water

1 Cook the onion in the butter or margarine.
2 Add the soup, vinegar and chutney. Gradually stir in the water, bring to the boil and simmer for 5 - 10 minutes.
3 Serve with bacon, ham or meat.

Cocktail or Sherry Parties

For a sherry party

Provide a choice of at least two different sherries, one medium dry and one dry. And if possible serve a sweet sherry too. Dry sherries are at their best slightly chilled, the flavour of the sweeter sherries is best at room temperature. Allow 1 bottle for 6 people at a 'sherry only' party. It is a good idea to have some tomato juice, chilled if possible. Dry sherry topped up with tomato juice makes a refreshing drink and is appreciated by guests keeping an eye on their calories.

For a cocktail party

Allow 3 - 4 short drinks, etc., and two long drinks per person. A cocktail or sherry glass holds about ⅛ pint. A tumbler for long drinks holds about ½ pint.

For 25 guests, the shopping list for drinks might be based on the following:

2 bottles gin
1 bottle Italian vermouth
1 bottle French vermouth
1 bottle lemon cordial.
1 bottle orange cordial
½ bottle Angostura bitters
½ bottle maraschino cherries.
½ bottle olives
2 - 3 lemons
2 - 3 packets cocktail sticks.

Plenty of ice is essential, and a siphon of soda and some bottles of tomato juice should be also provided. If you are planning to serve some elaborate cocktails, a selection of spirits will be required. Most people have their own ways of making cocktails, but in case you are a beginner, recipes for several standard ones are given here in this chapter.

The food served at both types of parties is similar:

Keep it 'bite size'—crisps, salted nuts and cheesy biscuits are all that is necessary, but if you have time to prepare some of these home made savouries, your guests will enjoy them. The dips can be made in a few minutes and will improve if left for several hours in a cold place.

Cocktail recipes

Gin and vermouth

Mix together equal quantities of Italian or French vermouth and dry gin, strain and serve.

The proportions of this drink may be varied to suit individual tastes.

Sweet martini cocktail

You require: 2 parts gin, 1 part Italian vermouth, 1 part French vermouth, sugar syrup, cocktail cherries. Mix the gin and vermouth, adding a few drops of the sugar syrup for each cocktail. Mix thoroughly and serve with a cherry in each glass.

Pink gin

You require: Angostura bitters and dry gin.
Put 2 - 3 drops of Angostura bitters into a cocktail glass and turn the glass so that the bitters run round the inside. Quickly turn the glass upside down to drain off any surplus and fill up with gin.

Gin rickey

You require: 1 wineglassful gin, 2 teaspoonfuls lemon juice, ice chips, soda water.
Mix together the gin and lemon juice, pour mixture over ice chips and fill up with soda water.

Onion dip

you will need:

2 3-oz. packets cream cheese spread	dash paprika pepper
2 tablespoons milk or cream	1 teaspoon anchovy essence (optional)
1 tablespoon lemon juice	potato crisps
1 teaspoon finely grated onion	

1 Cream the cheese until smooth. Add lemon juice to the milk or cream and gradually add to the creamed cheese.
2 Work in the onion and pepper and the anchovy essence if used. Mix thoroughly and turn into a serving dish.
3 Serve with potato crisps.

Pink dip

you will need:

2 3-oz. packets cream cheese spread	pinch salt
1 dessertspoon salad cream	potato crisps
1 tablespoon tomato ketchup	

1 Mix the salad cream and ketchup together.
2 Cream the cheese until smooth, gradually work in salad cream mixture.
3 Add the salt, mix thoroughly and turn into a serving dish.
4 Serve with potato crisps.

Cucumber dip

you will need:

2 3-oz. packets cream cheese spread
1 heaped tablespoon finely chopped unpeeled cucumber (well-drained)
few drops Worcestershire sauce
garlic salt
assorted cocktail biscuits
slices raw carrot
flowerets cauliflower

1 Cream the cheese until smooth.
2 Work in the cucumber, Worcestershire sauce and garlic salt. Blend together thoroughly.
3 Serve with assorted cocktail biscuits, thin slices raw carrots and flowerets of cauliflower.

Quick cheese straws

Cut a loaf of day-old bread into half-inch slices and remove the crusts. Cut the bread into 3-inch lengths, dip in melted butter and toss in grated cheese, to coat thoroughly. Place on a baking tray and brown for 15 - 20 minutes in a hot oven. Serve hot. If liked, the 'straws' can be rolled in crushed walnuts when they come out of the oven.

Party rolls

Wrap thin slices of ham round fingers of cheese and thread through a pineapple ring. Serve very cold on a plate lined with watercress.

Ham and nut puffs

cooking time 10 minutes
you will need:

½ pint milk
2 oz. fine semolina
2 egg yolks
4 oz. lean ham or boiled bacon (finely chopped)
2 oz. walnuts (finely chopped)
1 teaspoon made mustard seasoning
1 egg white (stiffly whisked)

1 Heat the milk, add the semolina and cook, stirring all the time until the mixture comes to the boil and thickens.
2 Simmer gently for 2 minutes, remove from the heat and stir in the egg yolks, ham, walnuts and mustard. Fold in egg white.
3 Season to taste with salt and pepper.
4 Drop heaped teaspoons of the mixture into hot deep fat or oil and fry for about 1 minute, until golden brown all over.
5 Drain on crumpled absorbent paper.
6 Serve hot, spiked on to cocktail sticks.
Makes about 3 dozen puffs.

Savoury éclairs (see page 72)

Fillings for savoury éclairs

Minced or finely chopped chicken and ham in a well seasoned white sauce.
Cream cheese blended with anchovy paste and chopped parsley.
Cream cheese blended with chopped chives.
Chopped hard-boiled eggs and capers in a white sauce.

Camembert canapés

Spread squares or cubes of toast with butter. Cut Camembert cheese into pieces the same shape as the toast but smaller. Put the cheese on the toast and place under a hot grill for a few minutes so that the cheese is just melted. Sprinkle with paprika and serve at once.

Devilled sardines

Drain a can of sardines, place on a plate. Sprinkle with the juice of a lemon, a little finely chopped onion, salt and cayenne pepper. Cover and leave in a cool place for at least an hour. Drain and dry the fish, toss in flour. Fry in hot oil until brown. Place on fingers of toast. Garnish with lemon butterflies and parsley. Serve at once.

Roe savouries

Remove roes from the tin, taking care not to break them.
Drain roes, toss in seasoned flour. Fry in butter until golden.
Arrange on fingers of hot buttered toast, sprinkle with paprika pepper and serve at once.

Sardine rarebit

Drain a can of sardines. Place 1 or 2 on each finger of buttered toast.
Pour a little rarebit mixture over each. Brown under a hot grill.

Mushroom and shrimp bouchées

1 dozen bouchée cases (see page 42)
1 packet mushroom white sauce mix
1 4-oz. can shrimps

Make up the mushroom white sauce mix as directed on the packet. Add the shrimps. Fill the bouchée cases. Place on a baking tray and put in a moderately hot oven (375° F.—Mark 5) for 15 minutes to heat through.

Ham and pineapple Bouchées

1 dozen bouchée cases (see page 42)
1 packet parsley sauce mix
4 - 6 oz. cooked ham (chopped)
little chopped pineapple

Make up the parsley sauce as directed on the packet. Add the ham and pineapple. Fill the bouchée cases. Place on a baking tray and put in a moderately hot oven (375° F.—Mark 5) for 15 minutes to heat through.

Coffee Party

Having friends in for coffee, either in the morning or in the evening, is a simple way of entertaining, ideal for those who do not want to give elaborate parties.

For morning coffee, any kind of biscuits, scones or small cakes can be served. At an evening coffee party, however, your guests will probably have had a meal and the 'eats' should be small and dainty. Éclairs, petits fours, shortbread fingers and meringues are all suitable and anything made with plain chocolate is particularly good with coffee. So—try serving fingers of your favourite chocolate cake or biscuits coated with melted chocolate.

Rich chocolate cake

cooking time 45 - 50 minutes

you will need:

3 oz. plain chocolate	4 oz. butter
8 level tablespoons honey	3 oz. castor sugar
6 oz. plain flour	1 teaspoon vanilla essence
1 level teaspoon	2 eggs
bicarbonate of soda	scant ¼ pint water
¾ teaspoon salt	

1 Grease and line the bottom of two 8-inch sandwich tins.
2 Place chocolate and honey in small basin over pan of hot water. Stir until chocolate has melted, beat well and leave to cool.
3 Sieve flour and bicarbonate of soda and salt together 3 times.
4 Cream butter, beat in sugar, continue beating until light and fluffy.
5 Beat in chocolate mixture, then eggs one at a time. Add vanilla essence.
6 Stir in flour a little at a time, alternately with water.
7 Beat well and divide mixture between the tins.
8 Bake in a moderate oven (350° F.—Mark 4). Cool slightly before turning out of the tins.

Honey chocolate icing

you will need:

6 oz. plain chocolate	2 tablespoons warm water
4 level tablespoons honey	8 oz. icing sugar

Place chocolate and honey in a small basin over a pan of hot water. Stir until chocolate has melted, remove from pan and allow to cool slightly. Beat in half the sugar, stir in the water and remaining sugar. Beat well. Spread one cake with icing and place second cake on top. Coat top and sides of cake with icing, roughing up with knife into swirls.

Bourbon biscuits

cooking time 10 - 15 minutes

you will need:

6 oz. flour	few drops vanilla essence
2 oz. cocoa	chocolate cream filling or
4 oz. butter	melted chocolate
4 oz. castor sugar	castor sugar
1 egg yolk	

1 Sieve the flour and cocoa.
2 Rub in the fat until the mixture resembles breadcrumbs.
3 Stir in the sugar.
4 Add the egg yolk and the essence and mix to a firm dough, adding a little water if necessary.
5 Roll dough out thinly and prick all over with a fork. Cut into strips 3 inches by ¾ inch.
6 Place on a greased baking tray and bake in a hot oven (400° F.—Mark 6).
7 Leave on a wire tray until cold. Sandwich together with cream filling or melted chocolate.
8 Dust each lightly with a little castor sugar.

Brandy snaps

cooking time 7 - 10 minutes

you will need:

2 oz. butter or margarine	½ teaspoon ground ginger
2 oz. sugar	1 teaspoon brandy or
2 tablespoons golden syrup	rum essence
2 oz. flour	½ teaspoon grated lemon
	rind
	¼ pint double cream

1 Grease 2 baking sheets.
2 Sieve flour and ginger.
3 Melt fat, sugar and syrup over a gentle heat until sugar has dissolved.
4 Remove from the heat, beat in flour and flavouring.
5 Drop in teaspoonfuls 2 inches apart on a tray.
6 Bake in a moderate oven (350° F.—Mark 4).
7 Meanwhile grease 2 or 3 wooden spoon handles.
8 Remove tray from oven and leave in a warm place so that the snaps cool without becoming too hard.
9 Remove from the tray one at a time using a palette knife, and roll round a wooden spoon handle. Leave in a cool place until firm. Slip off the handle carefully.
10 Shape each in the same way and pipe whisked double cream into the end of each when cold.
11 If snaps become too hard to roll, pop the tray back into the oven for 1 - 2 minutes to soften the mixture.

Chocolate kisses
cooking time 15 minutes
you will need:

4 oz. butter	1 dessertspoon cocoa
1 oz. icing sugar	vanilla butter cream
3½ oz. flour	

1 Sieve the flour and cocoa.
2 Cream the fat and sugar.
3 Gradually beat in the flour and cocoa.
4 Put mixture into a forcing bag fitted with a large star nozzle.
5 Pipe in whirls on a greased baking sheet.
6 Bake in a moderately hot oven (375° F.—Mark 5).
7 Cool on a wire tray.
8 When cold sandwich together in pairs with butter cream.

Truffle cakes
you will need:

4 oz. stale sponge cake	almond or rum essence
4 oz. castor sugar	(optional)
4 oz. ground almonds	chocolate glacé icing or
apricot jam	melted chocolate
	chocolate vermicelli

1 Grate the cake into crumbs or rub through a coarse sieve into a mixing bowl.
2 Add the sugar and almonds.
3 Warm the jam over a gentle heat and sieve.
4 Blend the cake and almond mixture to a firm paste with the jam, adding a few drops almond or rum essence if liked.
5 Shape the mixture into 12 - 18 balls and leave to become firm in a cool place.
6 Dip each ball in a glacé icing or melted chocolate using a skewer.
7 Roll in chocolate vermicelli and leave on a plate to dry.
8 Serve in small paper cases.

Marzipan petits fours
cooking time 20 minutes
you will need:

4 oz. ground almonds	2 egg yolks
4 oz. castor sugar	cherries or angelica or
almond essence	halved walnuts

1 Grease a baking tray lightly and cover with a piece of rice paper.
2 Mix the almonds, sugar and a few drops almond essence.
3 Stir in sufficient egg yolk to bind to a stiff paste.
4 Turn the paste on to a surface dusted with castor sugar. Dredge with more castor sugar and roll out about ½ inch thick.
5 Cut into small fancy shapes and decorate with halved glacé cherries or walnuts, or pieces of angelica. Place on the prepared tray.
6 Bake in a slow oven (310° F.—Mark 2) until lightly coloured and firm to the touch.
7 Allow to become cold on the tray. Cut rice paper to the shape of each cake.

Chocolate chip cookies
cooking time 10 minutes
you will need:

6 oz. flour	1 oz. brown sugar
½ teaspoon salt	1 egg
3 oz. butter	vanilla essence
3 oz. granulated sugar	4 oz. plain chocolate

1 Sieve the flour and salt.
2 Cream the fat and sugars. Beat in the egg and essence.
3 Grate or chop the chocolate coarsely. Stir it into the creamed mixture with the flour.
4 Put in teaspoonfuls on a greased baking sheet and bake in a moderate oven (350° F.—Mark 4).
5 Place on a wire tray and leave until cold.

Coffee time cookies
cooking time 20 minutes
you will need:

2 oz. butter	pinch salt
2 oz. sugar	coffee glacé icing
½ beaten egg	18 walnut halves
4 oz. flour	

1 Sieve the flour and salt.
2 Cream the fat and sugar and beat in the egg.
3 Stir in the flour.
4 Turn the dough on to a lightly floured surface.
5 Roll out ⅛ inch thick and cut into 2-inch rounds.
6 Place on a baking sheet. Bake in a moderate oven (350° F.—Mark 4). Cool on a wire tray.
7 When cold, coat the top of each with coffee glacé icing and place a walnut half on each.

Chocolate topsies
Make as above, spread cold cookies with melted chocolate and sprinkle with desiccated coconut.

Snow drops
Make as above. When cold, sandwich together with raspberry jam. Coat with glacé icing and sprinkle thickly with desiccated coconut.

Chocolate fingers
Make dough and roll out as above. Cut into fingers 2½ inches long. Bake for 20 minutes. When cold, dip ends of each biscuit in melted chocolate.

Scotch shortbread
cooking time 30 - 40 minutes
you will need:

6 oz. plain flour	2 oz. castor sugar
2 oz. cornflour	½ egg yolk
4 oz. butter	

1 Sieve the flour and cornflour into a bowl.
2 Rub in the butter and sugar.
3 Stir in the egg yolk and work all well together.
4 Turn mixture on to a floured surface and knead well until mixture is smooth and free from cracks.
5 Shape mixture into a round cake. Mark all round the edge with the back of a fork.
6 Prick the centre lightly with a fork.
7 Bake in a slow oven (335° F.—Mark 3).
8 Lift carefully on to a wire tray, sprinkle with castor sugar and leave until cold.

Shortbread fingers

Make mixture as above. Roll out into an oblong. Cut into fingers and prick down the centre of each. Place on a baking tray and bake for 15 - 20 minutes at 350° F.—Mark 4. Cool on a wire tray and sprinkle with castor sugar.

Lemon coconut cookies

cooking time 8 - 10 minutes
you will need:

4 oz. butter or margarine	pinch salt
1 oz. icing sugar	lemon curd
½ teaspoon vanilla essence	coconut
4 oz. plain flour	

1 Sieve the flour and salt.
2 Cream fat and sugar, adding the essence.
3 Stir in the flour and mix well.
4 Take 1 level dessertspoon dough for each cookie and form into a ball, flatten slightly.
5 Place the cookies 1 inch apart on an ungreased baking tray.
6 Bake in a hot oven (400° F.—Mark 6) until lightly browned.
7 Cool on a wire tray.
8 Spread lemon cream or lemon curd on each cookie and sprinkle with desiccated coconut.

Lemon cream

Beat 1 egg slightly in a basin over a small pan of hot water. Add the finely grated rind of 1 lemon, 6 oz. castor sugar, 3 tablespoons lemon juice and 1½ tablespoons butter. Stir and cook over hot water until well blended and thick. Allow to cool.

Chocolate orange cookies

Make as above. Top the cookies with orange flavoured glacé icing and sprinkle with grated chocolate. Leave in a cool place until dry.

Almond cookies

Make as above, replacing vanilla with almond essence. Press half a blanched almond in the centre of each cookie before baking.

Favourite cookies

Make as above, replacing vanilla with lemon essence. Coat cookies with thick white glacé icing and place a halved glacé cherry in the centre of each. Leave in a cool place to dry.

Meringues

cooking time 3 - 4 hours
you will need:

3 egg whites	3 oz. granulated sugar
pinch salt	3 oz. castor sugar

1 Turn two baking trays upside down and cover with greaseproof paper brushed lightly with oil.
2 Place egg whites in a deep bowl, add the salt.
3 Whisk with a wire whisk or a rotary beater until stiff and 'dry'.
4 Lightly fold in the granulated sugar and continue whisking until mixture regains its former stiffness.
5 Fold in the castor sugar (do not disturb mixture more than necessary).
6 Spoon mixture into a large forcing bag fitted with a plain nozzle and pipe in rounds or cones on to the prepared tins.
7 Dredge with castor sugar and bake in a very slow oven until firm and crisp. Do not allow to brown.
8 Remove tray from oven. Slide each meringue off the tray by slipping a knife underneath each. Place on a wire tray until cold. (When cold, meringues can be stored several weeks in a tin).
9 Sandwich meringues together with whipped cream or butter cream just before serving.

Note:
Have egg whites as fresh as possible and keep in a cold place until ready to make meringues. If a forcing bag is not available, have 2 dessertspoons in a jug of cold water handy for shaping the meringues. Take up a good spoonful of the mixture in one spoon, smooth it into shape with the second spoon and lay it on the prepared tin.

Meringue à la Chantilly

Make the meringues as above. Sandwich together with double cream whisked until thick and flavoured with vanilla essence. A little castor sugar may be added to the cream if liked.

Cherry meringues

Make meringues as above. Whisk cream until thick and fold in chopped glacé cherries. Flavour with a little cherry brandy if available.

Almond meringue fingers

Make the meringues as above, adding a few drops almond essence to the egg whites. Pipe the meringues in finger lengths on a tin prepared as above. Sprinkle with toasted almonds, roughly chopped and make in a slow oven until firm and crisp. When cold sandwich with butter cream.

Fruit filled meringues

Make meringues as for plain meringues. Pipe mixture in rings, piping two or three rings, one on top of the other to form 'nests'. Bake as for plain meringues. When meringues are required, fill with fresh or drained canned fruit and decorate with whipped cream.

Making coffee

The jug method is the easiest and one of the best methods. For every pint of water, you need 2 heaped tablespoons coffee (fine ground).

1 Heat jug by filling it with boiling water and allowing it to stand for about 5 minutes.
2 Empty jug and dry it.
3 Put the coffee in jug and pour on boiling water, stirring vigorously.
4 Leave jug in a warm place for 5 minutes, stirring once or twice.
5 Leave without stirring for a further 5 minutes. The coffee is then ready to serve. If there appear to be too many grounds on the top, lightly skim these off with a spoon, or carefully pour off one cup of coffee, and then pour back into jug. This will cause grounds to settle.

If you are serving the coffee in another pot, make sure that the pot is really hot. If it is necessary to reheat the coffee, take care that it does not boil.

Children's Parties

Invitations should be sent out about a fortnight before the appointed day, and most children enjoy receiving coloured picture invitation cards, with acceptance forms attached which they can fill in themselves.

As soon as you know the number you may expect, decide on the menu and make out a shopping list. Here are some reminders:
Silver balls, sweets, cherries, etc., for cake decorations.
Cake candles and cake candle holders.
Paper serviettes.
Drinking straws.
Waxed cases for jellies and ice cream.
Doilies.
Balloons and paper hats.
Coloured wrapping paper and fancy string.
A small present for each guest when they leave, and one or two prizes for games.

Small children do not notice the finer points of furniture or flower arrangement, but they do need space, so push back all the furniture against the walls. Make sure any open fire is properly guarded. Have a damp flannel and towel within easy reach for the little ones who are inclined to get very sticky at tea time.

Do not forget that the 'Mums' will be calling to collect the children, so have tea or coffee, bridge rolls or sausage rolls, and some small cakes—or a slice of your best fruit cake—ready to offer.

For very small children

Children are usually too excited to eat a great deal, and it is normally only necessary to allow about six items of food per head; three plain or savoury and three sweet. It is a good idea to provide cardboard plates and cups, since these are easier for small children to handle and there is no danger of your china being broken.

Sandwiches. Make sandwiches with chopped hard-boiled eggs and chopped tomato, grated cheese, thinly sliced luncheon meat or ham, mashed bananas or grated apple and grated chocolate mixed. Cut sandwiches out with small round cutters or cut into squares or triangles, cutting off the crusts.

Open Sandwiches. Spread slices of bread with honey, jam or paste, lemon curd or chocolate spread. Cut into squares, removing the crusts.

Cheese and biscuits. Serve cubes of mild flavoured cheese with small semi-sweet biscuits or fingers of bread and butter.

Jam tarts. Sponge fingers. Biscuits.

Jelly. Serve in brightly coloured cartons, sprinkle with hundreds and thousands.

Ice cream (alternative to jelly). Serve vanilla ice cream, scooped into cartons, decorated with a glacé cherry and accompany with wafers cut into strips.

Birthday cake. Make a Victoria or sponge mixture in a Swiss roll tin. When cold, coat with glacé icing, pipe birthday greetings in butter cream and decorate with small chocolate animals or coloured sweets and candles.

Alternatively, mark the icing with a sharp knife, dividing the cake into the same number of slices as there are children. Pipe over these lines and pipe each child's name on a piece of cake, decorate each with a candle.

Menu for 5 - 10 year olds

Sandwiches or bridge rolls with savoury fillings
Sausages on sticks: cut cooked chipolatas in half and serve hot or cold
Alternatively, serve whole cocktail sausages
Cheese and biscuits
Potato crisps
Small scones: serve hot, if possible, spread with butter
Serve small dishes of strawberry jam and honey separately
Currant buns. Cut in half, toasted, if liked, and spread with butter
Jam and lemon curd tarts
Doughnuts
Chocolate biscuits
Ice cream with canned fruit
Birthday cake: Make three rounds of Victoria or sponge mixture, sandwich layers together with butter cream, and coat top with glacé icing. For a girl, decorate cake with flowers, coloured ribbon and candles. For a boy, decorate with 'match box' toys, cars, etc.

Menu for 10 - 12 year olds

A menu similar to that for the 5 - 10 year olds may be followed, but you may find that an early supper or buffet style party is more popular. Increase the quantity of food, remembering that the modern schoolchild prefers savoury foods to sweet. Sausage rolls, hamburgers and hot dogs are all popular with this age group, simple kebabs made with cubes of cheese, pineapple and luncheon meat, a homely version of a fondue, or savoury dips with French bread or savoury biscuits will add that longed-for touch of sophistication. And since it would not really be a party without ice cream or jelly, include some special sweets, for example: ice cream with hot chocolate or butterscotch sauce; a bowl of trifle or a chocolate mousse (made with evaporated milk and a jelly—they'll never know); and, of course, a traditional birthday cake.

Menu for older children

Sausage rolls, sardine and cheese rolls
Savoury patties
Bridge rolls
Small kebabs—halved sausages, cubes of cheese
Crisps
Hamburgers or hot dogs
Cheese biscuits with cream cheese or slices of cheese
Doughnuts
Chocolate biscuits
Small iced cakes (iced slab of cake cut into squares)
Trifles
Ice cream and hot chocolate sauce

Drinks

With very few exceptions, children choose orangeade or lemonade in preference to milk, although a milk shake is sometimes accepted. It is a good idea to make up the squash in a big jug beforehand to save time.

Suggested sandwich fillings for a children's party

Egg and tomato: Chop 2 hard-boiled eggs, skin and chop 2 tomatoes, blend together, adding salt and pepper to taste. This is sufficient for spreading 4 slices of bread. Finely chopped mustard and cress may be used instead of tomato.

Cheese: Grate 8 oz. Cheddar cheese and blend with 3 tablespoons mayonnaise. For older children, add 2 tablespoons sweet pickle or sandwich spread. Sufficient for spreading 6 slices.

Sardine: Drain sardines, removing the tails, mash with a fork, season with lemon juice and pepper. Sufficient for spreading 4 slices.

Salmon: Drain and flake a 7¾-oz. can pink salmon, removing any large bones, blend with 3 tablespoons cold white sauce or thin cream, season to taste. Chopped, peeled cucumber may be added for older children. Sufficient for 6 slices.

Ham and spread: Mash 4 oz. minced or finely chopped ham or luncheon meat with a 4 oz. packet of cheese spread. Sufficient for 8 slices.

Cheese dip

you will need:

8 oz. grated Cheddar cheese	good pinch cayenne
about 8 tablespoons single	pepper
cream or top of the milk	salt to taste

1 Mix the cheese and cream or milk together to a soft consistency.
2 Season to taste with pepper and salt.
This is a basic cheese dip. Any one of the following flavourings can be added:
A pinch of curry powder and chutney.
Chopped watercress and finely chopped onion.
Chopped nuts (walnuts are particularly nice) and a dash of Worcestershire sauce.
Chopped sultanas and raisins.
Tomato purée and finely chopped onion.
Chopped ham or grilled bacon.
Chopped gherkins or capers.
Chopped, stoned olives, glacé cherries and a dash of Worcestershire sauce.

Cheese fondue

cooking time 20 - 30 minutes

you will need:

2 oz. butter	seasoning
1 pint milk	2 eggs
2 oz. breadcrumbs	fingers toasted bread or
8 oz. grated cheese	biscuits
(preferably Gruyère)	

1 Put the butter and milk into a saucepan and bring to the boil.
2 Add the breadcrumbs and grated Gruyère cheese, and season to taste.
3 Stir over a gentle heat until the cheese is melted, add a beaten egg, and mix well until thoroughly hot.
4 Serve on fingers of toasted bread or biscuits. Alternatively, put the fondue in a large bowl, and let each person dip his own toasted slice.

Oven hot dogs

cooking time 15 - 20 minutes

you will need:

6 thin slices white bread	French mustard
2 oz. butter	6 chipolata sausages

1 Cut the crusts from each slice of bread, roll the slices with a rolling pin to make them thin and even.
2 Spread each slice with butter, and smear very lightly with mustard.
3 Put a sausage on each slice of bread. Roll up the bread and fasten with a wooden cocktail stick.
4 Place on a baking tray and bake in a hot oven (400° F.—Mark 6). Serve hot.

Tartlets

Make 6 oz. shortcrust pastry (see page 68). Roll out thinly and cut into rounds with a fluted cutter a little larger than the patty tins being used. Line 12 - 15 patty tins with the pastry, pressing it well in with the fingers.

Jam or lemon curd tartlets

Half fill each with jam or lemon curd, and bake in a hot oven (400° F.—Mark 6) for 15 - 20 minutes.

Syrup tartlets

Half fill with a mixture of 2 large tablespoons warmed syrup, 2 tablespoons cake or breadcrumbs and the juice of ½ lemon. Bake as above.

Ring doughnuts

cooking time 5 - 8 minutes

you will need:

6 oz. self-raising flour	2½ tablespoons milk
½ level teaspoon mixed spice	2 oz. castor sugar
1 tablespoon blended	pinch salt
vegetable oil	oil for frying
1 egg	

1 Sieve flour, salt and spice into a bowl. Add sugar.
2 Beat the tablespoon oil, egg and milk together.
3 Stir into the dry ingredients and mix to a soft dough.
4 Turn dough on to a floured surface. Roll out ¼ inch thick.
5 Cut into rounds with a 3 inch cutter. Cut out centres forming rings, with a 1½ inch cutter.
6 Re-roll remaining pieces of dough.
7 Pour enough oil into a deep frying pan to fill it one-third full.
8 Heat oil to 365° F. (Cube of bread will become golden on one side in 30 seconds).
9 Fry doughnuts one at a time until golden, turning them frequently during cooking.
10 Remove from oil with a perforated spoon, leave on crumpled kitchen paper to drain.
11 Toss in castor sugar. Serve on a doily. Makes twelve.

Cinnamon rings

Make as above, omitting mixed spice. Toss rings in castor sugar mixed with a little powdered cinnamon.

Iced rings

Make as above, when cold, spoon thin white glacé icing (vanilla or lemon flavoured) over the rings. Serve when the icing has set.

Animal crackers

cooking time 10 - 12 minutes

you will need:

4 oz. self-raising flour	few drops vanilla essence
good pinch salt	1 dessertspoon beaten egg
1½ oz. butter	glacé icing and silver balls
1½ oz. sugar	for decorating

1 Sieve the flour and salt.
2 Cream the fat and sugar and add the essence.
3 Beat in the egg and add the flour.
4 Knead to a firm paste. Roll out on a floured surface.
5 Cut out with floured animal cutters and place on a greased baking tray.
6 Prick biscuits all over with a fork.
7 Bake at 335° F.—Mark 3 until lightly coloured. Allow to cool on the baking tray, then lift carefully on to a wire tray and leave until cold.
8 Spoon a little glacé icing on to each biscuit and spread with the back of a teaspoon to fill the shape. Press silver balls in place for eyes.

Traffic light biscuits

cooking time 10 - 15 minutes

you will need:

biscuit mixture as for	green colouring
animal crackers	red colouring
8 oz. apricot jam (sieved)	icing sugar (sieved)

1 Roll the dough about ⅛ inch thick. Cut into 24 pieces, 3 inches long and 1 inch wide.
2 Using a ¼ inch cutter, cut out 3 circles down the centre of 12 biscuits.
3 Place all the biscuits on a greased baking tray and bake on the middle shelf at 335° F.—Mark 3.
4 When the biscuits are cold, spread the plain pieces thinly with apricot jam and dredge the cut ones with icing sugar.
5 Sandwich the biscuits together.
6 Fill up the centre hole in each biscuit with apricot jam, using a teaspoon.
7 Divide the remaining jam in half. Colour one half red and the other half green.
8 Fill the top hole of each biscuit with red jam and the bottom hole with green.

Gingerbread men

cooking time 15 minutes

you will need:

10 oz. self-raising flour	3 heaped tablespoons
pinch salt	golden syrup
2 oz. margarine	currants
4 oz. castor sugar	glacé cherries
3 teaspoons ground ginger	

1 Grease 2 or 3 baking trays.
2 Sieve flour, salt and ginger.

3 Heat fat, syrup and sugar until melted.
4 Stir into the dry ingredients and mix well.
5 Leave until firm and cool enough to handle.
6 Shape into small figures and place on to the baking trays.
7 Mark eyes with currants and put a few currants down the 'body'. Use a small piece of cherry for the mouth.
8 Bake on the middle shelf at 335° F.—Mark 3.
9 Ease from tray with a palette knife and leave on a wire tray to cool.

Snow men—Make as above, coating cold gingerbread men with white icing or frosting. Sprinkle thickly with coconut. Finish with currants and cherries as above.

Giant currant cookies

cooking time 10 - 15 minutes

you will need:

4 oz. self-raising flour	grated rind 1 orange
4 oz. fine semolina	2 - 4 oz. currants
4 oz. butter	2 eggs
4 oz. castor sugar	about 1 tablespoon milk

1 Sieve the flour and semolina.
2 Rub in the butter until the mixture looks like fine crumbs.
3 Add sugar, orange rind and currants.
4 Stir in the beaten eggs and milk, mixing to a stiff dough.
5 Turn on to a well-floured surface and knead lightly.
6 Roll out thinly and cut into rounds with a large biscuit cutter—about 3 inches.
7 Place on a greased tray and bake in a moderately hot oven (375°F.—Mark 5) until crisp and golden.

Honeybee biscuits

cooking time 10 - 15 minutes

you will need:

4 oz. butter	4 oz. plain flour
2 level tablespoons honey	chopped glacé cherries or
¼ teaspoon vanilla essence	chopped toasted
	almonds

1 Cream butter and honey until light and fluffy, add vanilla essence and mix well. Add sieved flour gradually.
2 Flour hands and roll small amounts of mixture into balls of three sizes.
3 Place 3 balls together, one under the other on a greased baking sheet to form one biscuit.
4 Flatten slightly and sprinkle with chopped cherries or almonds.
5 Bake in a moderately hot oven (375° F.—Mark 5). Cool on a wire tray.

Sugar biscuits

cooking time 15 - 20 minutes

you will need:

6 oz. self-raising flour	4 oz. sugar
pinch salt	1 egg
1 oz. cornflour	vanilla essence
4 oz. butter	

1 Sieve the flour, salt and cornflour into a bowl.
2 Rub in the butter and add the sugar.
3 Beat the egg with a few drops of essence and stir into the flour.
4 Work to a firm dough. Roll out on a floured surface and cut into fancy shapes.
5 Place on a baking sheet and bake at 375° F.—Mark 5.
6 Leave on a wire tray to cool. Dust with castor sugar.

Chocolate biscuits

Make as above. Sprinkle the biscuits while they are still hot with grated chocolate and leave on a wire tray to cool and set.

Orange or lemon biscuits

Make as above, adding a little finely grated orange or lemon rind to the sieved flour. Coat the cold biscuits with orange or lemon glacé icing.

Spicy biscuits

Make as above, adding $\frac{1}{2}$ teaspoon mixed spice to the flour before sieving. Coat the cold biscuits with white glacé icing and decorate with a slice of preserved ginger.

Black eyed Susans

Make dough as above, roll out barely $\frac{1}{8}$ inch thick. Cut out with round fluted cutters. Cut a small hole in the centre of half the biscuits. Place these rounds on the whole biscuits, first brushing the bases with a little egg white or water. Place on a baking tray and bake in a moderately hot oven (375° F.—Mark 5) for 18 - 20 minutes. When cold, fill the centre of each with blackcurrant jam or jelly or melted chocolate.

Swiss tarts

cooking time 30 minutes

you will need:

4 oz. butter or margarine	icing sugar
1 oz. castor sugar	raspberry jam or glacé
2 - 3 drops vanilla essence	cherries
4 oz. flour	

1 Sieve the flour.
2 Cream the fat and sugar until light and fluffy, adding the vanilla essence.
3 Fold in the sieved flour.
4 Using a forcing bag and a large star nozzle, pipe the mixture into paper cases on a baking

sheet. Start at the centre of the bottom of each case and pipe with a spiral movement round the sides, leaving a shallow depression in the centre.

5 Bake at 375° F.—Mark 5. Cool on a wire tray.
6 When the tarts are cold, dust with icing sugar and fill centre with a teaspoon jam or a halved glacé cherry.

Coconut pyramids

cooking time 3 - 4 hours

you will need:

2 egg whites	5 oz. desiccated coconut
5 oz. sugar	glacé cherries

1 Grease a baking sheet. Cut small rounds of rice paper, if liked, about 2 inches in diameter and place on the baking sheet.
2 Whisk egg whites stiffly and fold in sugar and coconut. Tint half the mixture pink if liked.
3 Pile mixture on rounds of paper or on to the baking sheet. Form into pyramid shapes.
4 Bake in a slow oven (265° F.—Mark $\frac{1}{2}$) until touched with gold. Top each with a halved glacé cherry half way through the cooking time.
5 Cool on a wire tray. Trim rice paper if necessary.

Chocolate coconut pyramids

Make as above, omitting the cherries. Allow the pyramids to cool and then top each with a teaspoon melted chocolate. Allow the chocolate to run down the sides a little and set.

Madeleines

cooking time 20 minutes

you will need:

4 oz. butter	raspberry jam
4 oz. sugar	desiccated coconut
2 eggs	glacé cherries
4 oz. flour	

1 Grease 12 dariole tins and place on a baking sheet.
2 Sieve flour.
3 Cream fat and sugar.
4 Beat in eggs, adding a little flour.
5 Fold in the remaining flour.
6 Three-quarters fill each tin.
7 Bake at 375° F.—Mark 5 until risen and brown.
8 Turn out on to a wire tray and leave until cold.
9 Trim cakes so that they are even in size and level at the bottom.
10 Sieve jam and heat gently. Brush over each cake.
11 Roll each cake in desiccated coconut which has been sprinkled thickly over a sheet piece of paper or foil.
12 Dip a cherry in the jam and stick on the top of each Madeleine.

Party time cake

cooking time 12 - 15 minutes

you will need:

3 eggs	*Filling:*
1½ tablespoons milk	3 oz. butter
¼ teaspoon vanilla essence	3 tablespoons lemon curd
6 oz. castor sugar	6 oz. icing sugar (sieved)
6 oz. self-raising flour	1 dessertspoon hot water
1¼ teaspoons baking	glacé icing (see page 80)
powder	
3 oz. butter (melted)	

1 Whisk the eggs, milk and essence together in a bowl.
2 Gradually add the sugar.
3 Fold in the flour, sieved with the baking powder.
4 Stir in the melted butter lightly, making sure it is well blended in.
5 Divide the mixture between two well greased 7-inch sandwich tins.
6 Bake at 375° F.—Mark 5. Cool in the tins for 5 minutes before turning out.
7 *Filling:* Cream the butter and sugar, then add the lemon curd and hot water. Beat until smooth.
8 Sandwich the cakes together when cold with the filling, and coat the cake with glacé icing.

Speedy sponge buns

Grease and flour some patty tins. Whisk 2 eggs and 2 oz. sugar until thick. Fold in 2 oz. flour, sieved. Spoon a little of the mixture into each tin. Bake in a moderately hot oven (375° F.—Mark 5) for 8 - 10 minutes. When cool, sandwich together with lemon curd and spread tops with chocolate glacé icing.

Some extras

Toffee apples

Peel and core some small eating apples, brush each with lemon juice as soon as it is peeled, then brush well with melted butter. Roll in brown sugar and bake in a hot oven on a greased baking sheet for 10 minutes. Stick a toffee apple stick in each—allow to cool before serving.

Party Sweets

Raspberry cream

you will need:

1 block vanilla ice cream	¼ pint double cream
1 raspberry jelly	angelica
2 tablespoons fresh orange	
juice	

1 Cut the ice cream into small squares.

'Sweet dreams'

Serve at going-home time—older children may like mugs of soup if it is a cold night, or a non-alcoholic punch.

Heat 1 pint of milk, add 2 tablespoons drinking chocolate. Bring to the boil, add sugar to taste and pour into mugs. Do not over-fill, top each mug with a marshmallow and serve.

Homemade lemonade

Make a sugar syrup—put 8 oz. sugar in a pan with ½ pint water, heat until sugar is dissolved, stirring. Bring to the boil and boil for 5 minutes without stirring, leave until cold. Squeeze the juice out of 4 large lemons, strain into a jug, add cold water or soda water and sugar syrup to taste.

Cider cup

1 pint cider (non-alcoholic)	1 small thin skinned
1 pint ginger ale	orange
1 bottle lemon squash	cloves (optional)

1 Cut orange into thin slices, stud each slice with cloves if liked.
2 Place into a bowl, pour in all the other ingredients and leave in a cool place for 1 hour.
3 Add 2 pints water, taste the punch and add more water if it seems too strong.
Makes 12 good glasses.

Ginger cream

Fill tall glasses with ginger ale, top with a spoonful of vanilla ice cream and serve at once.

Fruit punch

¼ pint strong tea	½ pint sugar syrup (make
¼ pint orange juice	as for homemade
¼ pint lemon juice	lemonade)
¼ pint pineapple juice	thin slices orange and
1 pint ginger ale	lemon

1 Strain tea, mix with fruit juices, ginger ale and sugar syrup.
2 Leave in a cold place for 2 or 3 hours.
3 Serve garnished with thin slices of orange and lemon, add sprigs of mint if available.
Makes 8 good glasses.

2 Melt the jelly and make up to just under ½ pint with very hot water. Add the orange juice.
3 While hot, pour over the ice cream. Add a little red colouring and whisk until thick and creamy.
4 Pour into sundae glasses and leave to set.
5 Decorate with cream and angelica.

Dairy ice cream

you will need:

½ pint milk	1 dessertspoon vanilla
2 oz. sugar	essence
2 eggs	¼ pint double cream

1 Set the dial of the refrigerator to the coldest setting.
2 Heat the milk and sugar and pour on to the beaten eggs.
3 Return to the pan and cook over a gentle heat until the mixture thickens.
4 Remove from the heat and add the vanilla essence. Allow to become completely cold, but not set.
5 Half whip the cream and fold into the cold mixture.
6 Pour into containers and place in the freezing compartment until crystals begin to form.
7 Remove to a cool bowl and beat well. Replace in the containers and freeze. Serve with a sauce.

Coffee sauce

Blend together ½ pint strong black coffee and 3 level teaspoons arrowroot. Place in a small saucepan, bring to the boil and simmer gently for 2 - 3 minutes. Remove from the heat, cool slightly and stir in 2 heaped tablespoons sugar and 1 oz. soft margarine.

Caramel sauce

Place 4 rounded tablespoons soft brown sugar and 4 level tablespoons golden syrup in a pan. Heat and stir until dissolved. Bring to the boil and simmer for 2 minutes. Allow to cool. Add 2 oz. soft margarine and 4 tablespoons water. Return to the heat and boil for 2 minutes. Allow to cool again and then serve with ice cream.

Peppermint sauce

Blend together ½ pint milk and 2 level teaspoons arrowroot. Place in a small saucepan, bring to the boil and simmer gently for 2 - 3 minutes. Remove from the heat and cool slightly. Add 1 rounded tablespoon castor sugar, 1 oz. soft margarine, ¼ teaspoon peppermint essence and a few drops of green colouring.

Apricot sauce

you will need:

8 oz. fresh or canned apricots	lemon juice
¼ pint water or syrup from the can	1 teaspoon maraschino (optional)
1 - 2 oz. brown sugar	1 level teaspoon arrowroot

1 Stone the apricots (if fresh) and stew until soft in the water or juice.
2 Rub through a sieve.
3 Crack the stones, scald and skin the kernels.
4 Add the sugar, lemon juice to taste, liqueur (if used) and the kernels to the sieved apricots.
5 Reheat the sauce, stirring in the arrowroot blended with a little cold water. Bring to the boil and serve.

Butterscotch sauce

you will need:

4 oz. moist dark brown sugar	strip lemon rind
½ pint water	1 teaspoon arrowroot
1 oz. butter	few drops vanilla essence
	few drops lemon juice

1 Dissolve the sugar in the water over a gentle heat. Add the butter and lemon rind, boil for 5 minutes. Remove the lemon rind.
2 Blend the arrowroot with 2 teaspoons cold water and use to thicken the sauce.
3 Add vanilla essence and lemon juice to taste.

Carnival cream (or simple chocolate mousse)

you will need:

1 lemon jelly	1 small can evaporated
2 oz. plain chocolate	milk

1 Dissolve the lemon jelly in a little hot water.
2 Make up to ¾ pint with cold water.
3 Pour a little of the jelly into a 1½ pint size mould.
4 Leave the remaining jelly in a cool place until almost setting.
5 Meanwhile, melt the chocolate slowly and remove from the heat.
6 Whisk the evaporated milk (chilled if possible) until thick.
7 Add the almost setting jelly to the milk, whisking thoroughly.
8 Fold in the melted chocolate.
9 Pour into the mould and leave to set.
10 When set, turn out and decorate as liked.

Lemon cream jelly

you will need:

1 lemon jelly	1 teaspoon cornflour
1 8-oz. can fruit salad	1 tablespoon sugar
½ pint milk	cream
1 beaten egg	

1 Drain the juice from the fruit salad and make up to ½ pint with water.
2 Dissolve the jelly in a little hot water and add the juice. Cool.
3 Heat the milk and pour on to the beaten egg blended with the cornflour. Mix well.
4 Pour into the pan and stir over a gentle heat until thick.
5 Do not allow the mixture to boil.
6 Add the sugar and allow to cool.

7 Stir the jelly and half the fruit into the custard and pour into a mould. Leave to set.

8 When set, turn out and decorate with the remaining fruit.

9 Serve with cream.

Chocolate pear flan

cooking time about 5 minutes

you will need:

4 oz. plain chocolate	1 flan case (sponge or
1 small can evaporated	pastry)
milk	blanched almonds
1 can pear halves	(optional)

1 Break the chocolate into pieces into a bowl. Place over a pan of hot water.

2 When the chocolate begins to melt, stir in the evaporated milk.

3 Cook until thick and then allow to cool.

4 Meanwhile drain the pears well.

5 Arrange, cut side down, in the flan case.

6 Coat each pair half with the cooled chocolate sauce and decorate with almonds if liked.
The chocolate sauce is ideal to serve with ice cream. It can be used hot or cold. If a sweeter sauce is preferred, 2 - 3 oz. castor sugar may be added to the chocolate.

Harlequin sundaes

you will need:

1 red jelly	2 family bricks vanilla
1 yellow jelly	ice cream
1 small can peaches	2 oz. chopped walnuts
1 small can pears	¼ pint double cream,
1 small can pineapple	sweetened and whipped
melba sauce	maraschino cherries

1 Make up the jellies and when set, whip up with a fork.

2 Mix the fruit together and place a small amount in the bottom of tall individual glasses.

3 Cover this with about 1 tablespoon whipped jelly and cover the jelly with a scoop of ice cream. Coat the ice cream with melba sauce.

4 Repeat these layers again and sprinkle the sundaes with chopped nuts.

5 Decorate the tops with swirls of cream and top each with a cherry.

Melba sauce

Sieve the required quantity of fresh raspberries through a nylon sieve. Sweeten to taste with icing sugar and use as required.

Neapolitan sundaes

you will need:

1 block Neapolitan ice	1 teaspoon gelatine
cream	2 tablespoons castor sugar
1 small can cherries	red colouring
1 large banana	

1 Strain the cherries and make the juice up to ½ pint with water.

2 Dissolve the gelatine and sugar in the juice and tint with a little red colouring. Leave to cool.

3 Peel the banana and cut into slices. Mix with cherries and divide between sundae glasses.

4 Pour on the cooled jelly and leave to set.

5 Just before serving top each sundae with a scoop of ice cream.

Fruit sundae

you will need:

1 small brick vanilla ice	1 banana
cream	1 peach
1 small brick strawberry	2 oz. raspberries
ice cream	¼ pint double cream
2 oz. grapes	

1 Place a portion of vanilla and strawberry ice cream in individual dishes.

2 Peel the grapes, remove the seeds and mix with the peeled sliced banana, chopped peach and the raspberries.

3 Spoon some fruit mixture into each dish and decorate each with whipped cream, sweetened to taste.

Pear délice

you will need:

4 pear halves	¼ pint chocolate sauce
1 family brick strawberry	(see this page)
ice cream	1 oz. plain chocolate

1 Place a pear half, hollow side up, in 4 individual dishes.

2 Place a slice or scoop of ice cream on each pear and coat with hot chocolate sauce.

3 Sprinkle with grated chocolate and serve at once.

Banana sundaes

you will need:

6 bananas	¼ pint double cream
1 family brick vanilla ice	2 oz. chopped walnuts
cream	8 maraschino cherries
¼ pint melba sauce	
(see above)	

1 Peel the bananas and split in half lengthways. Put into individual dishes.

2 Put two small slices of ice cream between the bananas.

3 Coat the ice cream with melba sauce and sprinkle with chopped walnuts.

4 Decorate with whipped cream sweetened to taste, and cherries.

Wedding Reception or 21st Birthday Party

Sit-down Meal for Fifty

Catering for large numbers at home is a challenge, but provided you keep the menu simple, there need be no difficulties. Either plan to have a sit-down meal based on cold meat and salad, or prepare a buffet meal. This should contain small savouries and sandwiches, sausage rolls and savoury pastries. Serve a simple sweet, ice cream and fruit salad or a good trifle, wedding or 21st birthday cake. Finish with coffee. Champagne is the traditional drink for the toast on these occasions, but it may be replaced by a sparkling white wine such as a Moussec. It is usual to offer guests sherry when they arrive, and wine or a fruit cup or punch may be served with the food.

For fifty people you will need:

One 12 - 14 lb. turkey, one 14 lb. gammon, one or two ox tongues (average weight 4 lb.). Salad: ten medium sized lettuces, 3 lb. tomatoes, 3 lb. cooked beetroot, three cucumbers and five 15-oz. cans of potato salad. This can be served either on individual plates or arranged on large dishes and handed round. Five dozen bread rolls, 2 lb. butter.
Five 1-lb. 14-oz. cans of fruit salad. This may be served in individual waxed jelly cases. Serve a small scoop of ice cream on each. One gallon of ice cream will be enough. You can order this specially from ice cream merchants. It must be delivered at the right time if your refrigerator is not large enough to store it. If you have a large enough 'fridge, turn it to its coldest setting. Cook the turkey, gammon and tongue the day before, leave them to get quite cold overnight and carve them in the morning. It is most important to have a sharp, long-bladed knife. Carve the gammon to the bone in thin slices. Carve the breast of the turkey first, in thin slices including the stuffing. Carve the dark meat last. Carve all the meat on to a large enamel tray, then transfer it on to plates, giving each one a slice of turkey breast and gammon, ox tongue and a little dark meat. (Keep the scraps and untidy pieces of both gammon and turkey and use them up later.) The tongue should be sliced thinly.

The turkey

Before stuffing the bird, calculate the roasting time. Allow 25 minutes per pound for slow roasting, or 15 minutes per pound at normal roasting temperatures.

For the stuffing:

You require: 9 oz. freshly made white breadcrumbs, 4 oz. shredded suet, 3 level tablespoonfuls chopped parsley, a good pinch dried thyme, finely grated rind of 2 lemons, a good pinch of fresh ground black pepper, 2 level teaspoonfuls salt, 2 small eggs, about 4 tablespoonfuls milk.

For cooking:

½ lemon, 8 oz. fat bacon rashers, 2 oz. butter or dripping.
To make the stuffing:
1 Mix all the dry ingredients together.
2 Beat the eggs lightly, stir them into the dry ingredients with enough milk to bind the mixture.
3 Work your hands under the skin of the turkey as far along the breast as you can. Put the stuffing carefully into the neck end of the turkey, pressing it well into the bird and under the breast skin so that during the roasting, the stuffing will help to keep the breast moist. Make sure the stuffing makes the bird look well rounded.
4 Tuck the loose skin which covered the neck under the wings to keep the stuffing in place.
5 Rub the breast of the turkey with the cut lemon.
6 Smear the bird with fat and cover the breast with rashers of fat bacon. Put the bird in a roasting tin and cover it loosely with kitchen foil. Cook at 325° F.—Mark 3, or at 375° F.—Mark 5, the normal roasting temperature. There is no need to baste the turkey more than once or twice during the cooking, replace the kitchen foil before returning the bird to the oven.
7 30 minutes before the roasting time is up, uncover the turkey, remove the foil and the bacon, baste the bird well and put it back in the oven to brown nicely. The heat may have to be turned up slightly.

8 Lift the turkey out of the roasting tin and leave it on a large plate until it is cold.

Note: Slow roasting is recommended to ensure a succulent turkey.

Boiled gammon

you will need:

14 lb. gammon, 6 peppercorns, 2 bay leaves, about 2 oz. demerara sugar, dry breadcrumbs

1 Weigh the gammon and calculate the cooking time. Allow twenty minutes for each pound, add twenty minutes to the total.

2 Put the gammon into a large pan, cover it with cold water and leave for 12 hours or overnight.

3 Dry the gammon and scrape it over with the back of a knife to remove the 'bloom'. Rub the cut surface with demerara sugar and leave it to absorb the sugar for twenty minutes.

4 Put the gammon into a pan containing enough fresh cold water to cover it and bring slowly to the boil. (You might need to borrow a fish kettle or large preserving pan to cook the gammon.) Add the bay leaves and peppercorns.

5 Simmer slowly for the calculated time. Leave the cooked gammon in the pan until it is cool enough to handle. Remove from the pan, peel off the dark outside skin.

6 Dust the fat surface thoroughly with dry crumbs and leave the gammon until it is quite cold before carving.

Quantities for a Buffet Meal for 50 People

200 small sandwiches or bridge rolls	2 quartern loaves (1 loaf gives 50-60 slices), 2 lb. butter
100 small vols au vent or bouchées	2 lb. rough puff or flaky pastry
100 sausage rolls	1 lb. flaky or shortcrust pastry, 2 lb. sausages
100 cheese straws	8 oz. cheese pastry
200 canapés or small savouries	2 lb. shortcrust pastry to make base
100 chocolate éclairs	10 oz. flour, 1 pint cream for filling, 1 lb. icing sugar
100 petits fours	1½ lb. Victoria sandwich mixture baked in three Swiss roll tins
50 - 75 meringues	10 egg whites—1 pint cream
6 flans or lemon meringue pies	1 flan or pie of 8-inch diameter will give 8 small servings
6 quarts of jelly, cream or mousse type sweets	1 quart gives 8 - 10 servings
8 quarts of fruit salad	8 lb. fruit (1 quart serves 6)
celebration cake	
coffee	1½ lb. ground coffee, 12 pints each milk and water, sugar
10 - 12 bottles champagne or sparkling white wine	1 bottle gives 8 good glasses.

OR

12 quarts punch or fruit cup	1 quart serves 6
6 pints of tomato or fruit juice	1 pint serves 4

2 PINTS = 4 standard cups = 1 quart

Boiled ox tongue

you will need:

1 ox tongue	1 turnip
1 onion	bunch mixed herbs
1 carrot	stock

1 Wash the tongue and soak for at least 2 hours. If the tongue is dry or hard, soak for 12 hours.

2 Place the tongue in a large pan of cold water. Bring slowly to the boil, skim and add the vegetables and herbs. Simmer gently (30 minutes per pound and 30 minutes over).

3 When cooked, remove from the pan and remove the skin carefully.

4 Place the tongue in a bowl or flat tin and curl round tightly. Cover with stock, place on a saucer or plate and press with a heavy weight until cold, then turn out.

Cheese butterflies

cooking time 10 - 15 minutes

you will need:

4 oz. cheese pastry (see page 71)	little milk
	finely chopped parsley
cream cheese	or paprika pepper

1 Roll the pastry out thinly and cut into 12 small rounds. Cut six of the rounds in half.

2 Bake in a hot oven, 400° F.—Mark 6.

3 Leave on a wire tray until cold.

4 Mix the cheese to a piping consistency with the milk and pipe a large star on to each round of pastry.

5 Set two half-biscuits in the cheese to form wings, and decorate with chopped parsley or paprika pepper. Makes 12 savouries.

Sausage rolls

cooking time 15 - 20 minutes

you will need:

8 oz. flaky pastry (see page 69)	1 lb. sausages beaten egg

1 Make pastry.
2 Dip sausages in warm water, slit skins and remove.
3 Sprinkle palms of hands with flour, and form sausage into rolls about 14 inches long on a floured surface.
4 Roll pastry into a thin strip, trim off edges and divide into four pieces lengthwise.
5 Brush pastry lightly with egg and put a roll of sausage on each strip.
6 Roll up, press edges together securely, and cut each roll into 12 pieces.
7 Place on an ungreased baking sheet, brush the top of each with beaten egg, make 2 or 3 small cuts on the top of each roll.
8 Bake at 450° F.—Mark 8—until golden.
9 Leave to cool on a wire tray.
Makes 24 small rolls.

Bouchées or small vols au vent

cooking time 15 - 20 minutes

you will need:

1 lb. rough puff pastry using   beaten egg
  1 lb. flour (see page 69)   fillings

1 Roll out pastry ⅜ inch thick. Cut out rounds with a 1½-inches diameter cutter (about 44 rounds from first rolling of pastry).
2 With a ¾-inch cutter, cut through each round of pastry.
3 Place on baking sheets and leave in a cold place for 30 minutes.
4 Brush with beaten egg and bake at 450° F.—Mark 8—for 12 minutes.
5 Remove from oven. Scoop out centre of each patty case, using the handle of a teaspoon. Put trays back in the oven for about 4 minutes to dry out bouchées.
6 Re-roll trimmings of pastry, leave in a cold place for about 20 minutes and cut out remaining pastry cases and fifty small rounds for lids, using a ¾-inch cutter.
7 Leave in a cold place for half an hour.
8 Bake as above, removing lids after 8-10 minutes. Makes 50 bouchées.
These pastry cases may be made several days beforehand. Fill the night before, and heat through if possible before serving.

Fillings:

½ pint thick, white sauce, with one of the following added, will fill 25 bouchées

6 oz. picked shrimps, prawns or any other shellfish

2 chopped hard-boiled eggs and 2 oz. minced ham

4 oz. chopped or minced chicken and 2 oz. minced ham

2 peeled and cut-up tomatoes and 3 oz. finely grated cheese

4 - 6 oz. flaked, tinned or fresh salmon

4 oz. diced ham and 2 oz. tongue or cooked veal

Haddock tricornes

cooking time 10 - 15 minutes

you will need:

6 oz. cheese pastry (see page 71)	½ pint thick cheese sauce (see page 59)
8 oz. cooked smoked haddock	egg or milk for glazing

1 Make the cheese pastry and roll it out thinly. Cut into rounds 3½ - 4 inches in diameter.
2 Mix the flaked and boned haddock with the cheese sauce and place a spoonful of filling in the centre of each round.
3 Brush the outside edge with a little water, draw up over the filling and pinch together to form a three-cornered shape.
4 Brush with a little egg or milk and bake in a hot oven, 400° F.—Mark 6 until golden.
Makes 12 savouries.

Marguerites

you will need:

4 oz. finely chopped ham	12 small round biscuits or
2 tablespoons mayonnaise	pastry rounds
salt and pepper	2 hard–boiled eggs

1 Mix the ham, mayonnaise and seasoning together, and spread the mixture on the biscuits.
2 Separate the white from the yolk of the hard-boiled eggs and cut the white in pieces with a small cutter to represent petals.
3 Sieve the egg yolk and place in the centre of the ham mixture.
4 Arrange the 'petals' round the egg yolk.
Makes 12 savouries.

Anchovy twists

cooking time about 10 minutes

you will need:

flaky pastry (see page 69)	beaten egg
anchovy fillets	

1 Roll out the pastry cut into thin finger lengths.
2 Cut some washed and dried anchovy fillets in halves, lengthways.
3 Place a half on each piece of pastry and twist the fish fillet and pastry together.
4 Put on to a baking tray, brush the pastry over with egg and bake in a hot oven (400° F.—Mark 6).

Stuffed celery sticks

Cut sticks of celery into even sized lengths and fill the centre of each with one of the following mixtures:

Minced chicken and cream sauce
Cream cheese and chopped nuts
Grated apple, chopped dates and walnuts
Sieved hard-boiled egg, butter and chutney
Chopped, cooked bacon and ham with piquant sauce

Simple canapés

Lightly spread savoury biscuits with butter and top with one of the following:

Cottage or cream cheese mixed with drained chopped pineapple. Decorate with a sprig of watercress
Peanut butter, topped with a piece of thinly sliced eating apple. Sprinkle well with lemon juice
Chopped hard-boiled egg mixed with mayonnaise, decorate with sliced stuffed chives or capers
Crab paste sprinkled with a few drops of lemon juice and decorated with a thin slice of cucumber. A slice of liver sausage topped with a little finely chopped onion or chutney
Cottage or cream cheese decorate with thin slices of preserved ginger
Grated raw apple, sprinkled with lemon juice and mixed with honey
Thin rounds from slices of processed cheese, decorated with lattice of drained anchovy fillets
Sardines mashed with a little vinegar or lemon juice decorated with a twist of lemon
Roughly chopped ham and raisins bound together with mayonnaise
Grated cheese mixed with chutney or sweet pickle topped with small rolls of cooked bacon or ham
Spread thinly with apple sauce and top with small pieces of crisply fried bacon
Cream or cottage cheese and a drained mandarin orange or marschino cherry
Crab meat moistened with tomato purée decorated with a lemon butterfly.
Grated cheese mixed with mayonnaise and topped with a pickled walnut or radish rose

Assorted canapés

Cut thin brown bread into fancy shapes and arrange on these: asparagus tips, smoked salmon, salami, etc., or pipe with a savoury butter. Make some aspic jelly according to instructions on packet, and spoon this over the canapés when the jelly is on the point of setting. Garnish with piped savoury butter, pieces of red pepper, etc.

Simple petits fours

Make a Victoria sandwich or sponge mixture (see page 73). Spread the mixture in a Swiss roll tin ($7\frac{1}{2}$ x $11\frac{1}{2}$ inches) which has been greased and lined. Bake in a moderately hot oven (375° F.—Mark 5) for 20 - 25 minutes. Turn out on to a wire tray and leave until cold. Trim the edges and cut the cake into 4 strips about 2 inches wide. Cut the remaining cake into 4 or 5 small rounds (using the trimmings of cake to make truffles).

Spread one strip of cake with sieved raspberry jam. Roll the cake in coconut. Cut into $1\frac{1}{4}$-inch pieces and decorate each with a halved glacé cherry and leaves of angelica.

Coat the second strip of cake with chocolate icing and sprinkle with chopped almonds. Cut into fingers.

Coat the top and sides of the third strip of cake with Vienna icing (see page 82). Cut into $1\frac{1}{4}$-inch fingers and decorate each with a halved walnut. Coat the fourth strip of cake with lemon flavoured glacé icing and decorate with segments of crystallised orange. Cut into fingers. Brush the tops of the rounds of cake with apricot jam, press a round of almond paste on to each. When set, pipe with butter cream.

Petits fours

you will need:

layer of Genoese sponge or Victoria sandwich (see pages 74, 73)	butter cream, made with 4 oz. butter (see page 80) glacé icing made with 12 oz. icing sugar (see page 80)

1 Flavour the butter cream with a few drops vanilla essence and tint to a pale pink with red colouring.
2 Cut the sponge into rounds $1\frac{1}{2}$ inches in diameter.
3 Pile butter icing on top of each round. Smooth with the back of a teaspoon to form a dome shape.
4 Place cakes on a wire tray over a large plate. Leave until the butter cream is firm.
5 Coat with white glacé icing. Allow the icing to run down the sides of the cake so that they are completely covered. The butter cream should just show through.
6 If liked, pipe with butter cream when the icing has set.
7 Serve the cakes in small paper cases.

Coffee for fifty people

It is recommended that an urn is borrowed or hired, otherwise the coffee may be made by the jug method (see page 21). Make sure that you have 3 or 4 large jugs available.

To make coffee in an urn:

Allow 1½ lb. finely ground coffee, infused in 8 - 10 pints of water (according to strength required), 10 - 12 pints of milk and 1½ lb. of loaf sugar.

Be sure that the urn is perfectly clean. Scald it, then rinse thoroughly with cold water. Put in the required amount of water and bring it to the boil. Add the coffee, tied loosely in a muslin bag or bags. Cover the urn, and stand it where the water will be kept hot without boiling. Allow it to infuse for 15 minutes, stirring the bags round occasionally. The coffee is then ready to serve.

If possible, heat the milk only as required, but if any has to be kept hot, stand it in hot water, covering it to prevent a skin forming. Strain the milk if there is any trace of skin.

Christening Party

A Christening party is usually a 'tea party' which is held after the church service. The food should be simple. Choose items that can all be prepared in advance and set the table before you go to church.

It is traditional to have a rich fruit cake appropriately iced and decorated as the highlight of the tea. It is usual to drink the health of the baby when the cake is cut. Champagne or a sparkling white wine is the accepted drink for this occasion.

The food for the tea may be based on the following:

Neapolitan sandwiches or sandwich loaf
Bridge rolls with savoury fillings
Scones
Biscuits
Iced sponge fingers
Sherry trifle
Lime mousse
Christening cake
Tea
Orange squash if there are children at the party

Neapolitan sandwiches

Prepare thin bread and butter, both brown and white, and three or four savoury fillings of contrasting colours, e.g. tomato, liver pâté, watercress and egg. Spread a piece of the bread and butter with one of the fillings and cover with a second piece of bread, buttered side down. Now butter the top, spread with one of the other fillings and cover with a third piece of bread and butter. Continue in this way, building up a large block of alternate layers of bread, butter and filling, working the different colours in rotation. Cut off the crust and press well. Wrap the whole block in foil or waxed paper and leave in a cool place for some hours with a weight on top. When required, cut into slices across the filling, making sandwiches of many-coloured stripes. Arrange the sandwiches on a plate to show the striped effect.

Party sandwich loaf

Suggested fillings:

Cream cheese spread, made with 8 oz. cream cheese, 4 oz. margarine, seasoning and pink colouring

Liver sausage spread, made with 6 oz. liver sausage, 4 oz. luxury margarine, seasoning

Sardine and curry spread, made with 1 can sardines, 4 oz. luxury margarine, 1 rounded teaspoon curry paste, seasoning

Cottage cheese spread, made with 8 oz. cottage cheese, 4 oz. luxury margarine, seasoning.

To make the filling:

Place ingredients in a mixing bowl and mix together until smooth. Select one of above fillings to make the sandwich loaf.

To make the party loaf:

Slice 1 large white loaf thinly lengthwise. Spread the slices with the chosen filling and put slices together to form a multi-layered loaf. Trim edges with a sharp knife. Coat top and sides—not ends—with filling and cover all over with peanuts. Place on serving plate and decorate with a sprig of parsley and black grapes.

German biscuits

cooking time 10 - 15 minutes

you will need:

4 oz. flour	red currant jelly
2½ oz. butter	white glacé icing (see page 80)
1 oz. castor sugar	glacé cherries

1 Sieve the flour into a bowl. Rub in the fat and add the sugar.
2 Knead the mixture by hand until it forms a smooth dough.
3 Roll out and cut into rounds with a small cutter or wine glass.

4 Bake in a slow oven (335° F.—Mark 3) until lightly coloured.
5 Place on a wire tray until cold.
6 Spread half the biscuits with red currant jelly and cover with the remaining biscuits.
7 Ice the top of the biscuits with white glacé icing and place a piece of cherry in the centre of each.

Coffee German biscuits

Make as above, icing with coffee glacé icing and placing a halved walnut in the centre of each.

Lemon German biscuits

Make as above. Sandwich together with lemon curd, ice with chocolate glacé icing and place a halved blanched almond in the centre of each.

Macaroons

cooking time 20 - 25 minutes

you will need:

2 egg whites	1 teaspoon orange flower
4 oz. ground almonds	water (optional)
8 oz. castor sugar	blanched whole almonds
1 oz. ground rice	egg white to glaze

1 Whisk the egg whites until stiff.
2 Stir in the ground almonds, sugar, ground rice and orange flower water, if used. Mix well.
3 Grease a baking tray and cover with a sheet of rice paper.
4 Spoon the mixture on to the tray in little heaps, leaving space between each.
5 Place a split blanched almond in the centre of each.
6 Bake in a moderate oven (350° F.—Mark 4) until pale gold in colour.
7 Leave on the tray until firm and then cut round each biscuit, trimming the paper neatly. Place on a wire tray until cold.

Chocolate macaroons

Make as above, omitting the almond decoration. Coat the finished biscuits with melted chocolate.

Viennese shortcakes

cooking time 20 minutes

you will need:

4 oz. self-raising flour	2 oz. icing sugar
4 oz. plain flour	½ teaspoon vanilla essence
7 oz. butter	butter cream (see page 80)

1 Grease 2 baking sheets.
2 Sieve both the flours together in a bowl.
3 Cream fat and sugar, adding the vanilla essence.
4 Beat in the flour, working the mixture with a wooden spoon until smooth.

5 Put mixture into a forcing bag fitted with a large rose pipe.
6 Pipe mixture in circles or strips on to the trays.
7 Bake in a moderately hot oven (375° F.—Mark 5).
8 Cool on a wire tray. When cold, sandwich with butter cream.

Viennese fingers

Make as above, piping the mixture in strips about 2½ inches long. Sandwich the biscuits with butter cream and dip the ends in melted chocolate.

Viennese tartlets

Cut out rounds of plain biscuit mixture. Using a small nozzle, pipe Viennese shortcake mixture in a circle around the edge of each biscuit round. Bake in a moderately hot oven 375° F.—Mark 5) for 25 - 30 minutes. Fill the centre of the cold tartlets with lemon curd or raspberry jam. Dust with icing sugar.

Sponge fingers

cooking time 7 - 10 minutes

you will need:

2 oz. flour	2 eggs
2 oz. castor sugar	castor sugar to dredge

1 Grease and flour a tray of sponge finger tins.
2 Sieve the flour.
3 Whisk the eggs and sugar together in a basin over hot water until thick.
4 Fold in the flour.
5 Turn mixture into the tins, sprinkle well with castor sugar.
6 Bake at 425° F.—Mark 7—until golden and firm.
7 Turn out on to a wire tray to cool.

Lemon sponge fingers

Make as above and when cold sandwich biscuits together in pairs with lemon curd. Dip ends of each in lemon-flavoured glacé icing.

Danish delights

Make sponge fingers as above. Spread thick glacé icing over top of each biscuit and sprinkle thickly with chopped mixed peel.

Chocolate fingers

Make sponge fingers as above. Melt a 2-oz. bar plain chocolate in a cup. Dip each finger into the chocolate, allowing the chocolate to come half way up the finger. Stand the biscuits in a small basin or cup, plain side down, until dry.

Sponge drops

Make mixture as for sponge fingers, adding a few drops of vanilla essence to whisked eggs and sugar. Spoon the mixture into a forcing bag, fitted with a plain ½-inch nozzle. Pipe into rounds, well apart, on a greased, floured tin. Bake at 425° F.—Mark 7—for 7 - 10 minutes until lightly coloured. Lift carefully on to a wire tray. When cold, dredge with castor sugar or coat the top of each with a little glacé icing.

Lime mousse

you will need:

1 lime jelly	1 egg
¼ pint hot water	cream (optional)
milk	

1 Dissolve the jelly in the hot water. Allow to become cool.
2 Stir in enough milk to make up to 1 pint.
3 Separate the yolk from the white of the egg.
4 Pour the jelly on to the beaten egg yolk and mix well.
5 Whisk the egg white until stiff and fold into the jelly.
6 Pour into a mould which has been rinsed out in cold water.
7 Leave to set. When set, turn out and serve with cream, if liked.

Sherry trifle

you will need:

1 7–inch sandwich cake or 3 individual sponge cakes	2 - 3 tablespoons sherry
2 tablespoons raspberry jam	1 pint thick custard
1 medium sized can fruit salad	¼ pint double cream
	2 oz. blanched almonds
	glacé cherries and angelica

1 Spread cake with jam and cut into cubes, place in a large glass bowl.
2 Drain juice from fruit, mix juice and sherry and sprinkle over the cake. Arrange fruit, chopped if preferred, on the cake.
3 Pour cool custard over and leave until cold.
4 Whisk cream until thick, and pipe round the edge of the trifle.
5 Arrange almonds in small circles, to represent the petals of a flower, on the custard. Place a cherry in the centre of each and finish with leaves of angelica.
If liked, the almonds may be chopped and toasted and sprinkled over the custard.
Serves 8 - 10.

Mandarin trifle. Make as above, using a chocolate sandwich cake and mandarin oranges instead of fruit salad. Decorate trifle with grated chocolate instead of almonds.

Custard

3 level tablespoons custard powder
1 pint milk
2 rounded tablespoons sugar

1 Blend the custard powder with a little of the milk.
2 Bring the remaining milk to the boil.
3 Pour on to the blended custard, stirring all the time.
4 Rinse the pan with cold water, return the custard to the pan and bring to the boil over a gentle heat, stirring all the time. Boil for 2 - 3 minutes, add the sugar.
If cold custard is required, cover with a plate to prevent a skin from forming.

Christening cake

Bake a rich fruit cake in an oblong tin, approximately 8 by 5 inches.

1 Cover with white fondant icing, fix on to a cake board and leave to dry.
2 Pipe edges with royal icing, tinted to a pastel shade, to represent basket weave.
3 Roll out a piece of fondant icing into an oblong about two-thirds the size of the top of the cake. Mark into a diamond pattern with a pointed knife. This is to represent a quilt.
4 Form a small piece of fondant icing into a pillow and fix this into position in the centre of one end of the cake. Place the quilt in position. Tuck a very small doll under the quilt with just the head showing on the pillow.
5 Pipe the top and bottom end of the cot with royal icing, using a small shell nozzle and decorate with tiny bows of pink or blue baby ribbon.
6 A small frill of net may be fastened round the edge of the cot, if liked.

Dinner Party

Having people in to dinner, whether just a few friends or an important acquaintance or business contact, can be quite a nightmare. The secret of success is careful planning right down to the smallest detail. First work out the menu —the meal centres around the main course, so choose this first. Select two or more vegetables to go with it, and/or a salad, remembering the importance of colour and contrast in texture. Decide on the sweet course and then choose between a first course or cheese to finish up. It is not necessary to serve more than three courses—but try to make one dish rather special. Serve something you can really be proud of—it is a compliment to your guests. It really is not wise to try a new recipe when you have guests to dinner, unless you have rehearsed the dish a couple of times.

If your chosen first course is cold, it may be ready on the table, waiting for the moment when you and your guests are. You may choose to serve small savouries with a drink beforehand and start with the main course. Whichever way you plan the meal, the main course should be served at the table with vegetables and accompanying sauces handed round. The dessert should also be served at the table or if in individual glasses, it may be brought in and put at each place setting, after the main course is cleared. Coffee may be taken at the table or in another room. Serve black coffee with cream or hot milk separately. The following recipes are intended to give you ideas for dishes which would be suitable for a dinner party—but try to add your own individual touch with the garnishing and flavouring. Unless otherwise stated, these recipes will serve four people, but the quantities can be increased according to the number of guests.

To illustrate how a menu is 'built up', here are two menus for six people, composed around a similar main course dish. Both meals could start with melon and finish with lemon meringue pie, but choice of cooking method and accompaniments makes each completely different.

Roast fillet of beef

cooking time 45 minutes - 1 hour

you will need:

2 lb. fillet of beef	oven browned potatoes
butter or olive oil	baked tomatoes
watercress	

1 Brush beef with melted butter or oil.
2 Place on a rack in a roasting tin.
3 Cook in the centre of a slow oven (335° F.—Mark 3). Allow 45 minutes for an underdone joint, 1 hour for a joint that is medium rare in the centre.
4 Serve the meat on a hot dish, surround with baked tomatoes, garnish with watercress. Serve Maître d'hôtel or mustard butter and potatoes and green salad.

Oven browned potatoes

you will need:

2½ lb. potatoes	1½–2 oz. butter
salt and pepper	

1 Peel potatoes, boil in salted water until almost cooked.
2 Drain, cut into quarters, place in a shallow, buttered ovenproof dish.
3 Sprinkle with salt and freshly milled pepper, dot with butter.
4 Cook on the bottom shelf of the oven while the meat is cooking.
5 Transfer to the top shelf during the last 15 minutes to brown.

Baked tomatoes

cooking time 15 minutes

you will need:

6 large tomatoes	salt and pepper
butter	castor sugar
1 teaspoon finely chopped onion (optional)	

1 Cut tomatoes in half, place in an ovenproof dish.
2 Sprinkle with salt, pepper and sugar and onion if used.
3 Put a tiny piece of butter on each, cover with greased paper.
4 Cook on bottom shelf of oven when potatoes are moved up to brown.

Green salad

Wash lettuce, drain well and leave in a cool place for at least 1 hour before serving. Rub the inside of the salad bowl with a cut clove of garlic if liked. Make a French dressing by mixing 3 tablespoonfuls olive oil with 1 tablespoon wine vinegar, adding a pinch of salt and freshly milled pepper. Place lettuce in a bowl, spoon dressing over and toss leaves gently. The prepared salad may be served on individual plates.

Maitre d'hôtel butter

you will need:

2 teaspoons finely chopped parsley	1 teaspoon lemon juice
2 oz. butter	salt and pepper

Scald parsley in boiling water, dry and chop. Cream butter, adding a pinch of salt and pepper. Blend in the parsley, beat in lemon juice a drop at a time. Spread on a plate and leave in a cool place until firm. Cut into cubes or rounds with a small cutter and serve in a small dish with chips of ice if available.

Mustard butter

Blend 2 teaspoons French mustard with 2 oz. butter. Finish and serve as for maître d'hôtel butter.

Grilled steak

cooking time about 10 minutes

you will need:

1½ lb. fillet steak	watercress butter
oil or butter	6 large mushrooms
salt and pepper	potato balls
green salad	tomato salad

1 Cut meat into slices, beat with a rolling pin on either side.
2 Brush with oil or melted butter and sprinkle with salt and pepper.
3 Place under a hot grill, grill quickly on either side, reduce heat. Cook more slowly until cooked to required degree. A rare steak requires 3 - 4 minutes for each side. If it is necessary to cook the steaks in two 'batches' remove the cooked steaks on to a hot dish, keep in a warm place while the remainder are cooking. While the steaks are cooking, fry mushrooms and potato balls.

To serve: Top each steak with a mushroom and a pat of watercress butter. Pile potato balls round, serve green salad and tomato salad separately.

Fried mushrooms

Wash and drain and peel the mushrooms if necessary. Fry in melted butter or bacon fat for 10 - 15 minutes, drain on kitchen paper.

Potato balls

Have prepared beforehand, 2 lb. mashed potato flavoured with lemon rind. With well floured hands, form the potato into balls. Roll in flour, egg and breadcrumbs. Fry in hot oil or fat until golden, 4 - 5 minutes. Drain well.

Watercress butter

Scald 2 tablespoons watercress leaves in boiling water. Dry and chop finely. Cream the butter, adding the watercress and salt to taste.

Tomato salad

you will need:

6 large tomatoes	French dressing
salt and pepper	finely chopped chive or
castor sugar	onion (if liked)

Peel and slice tomatoes. Place in a single layer in a dish. Sprinkle with salt and pepper and sugar, and onion if used. Leave in a cool place for at least 30 minutes. Lift carefully into serving dish, and spoon a little French dressing over.

These steak dishes may also be served with duchesse or sauté potatoes and creamed spinach.

Quantities of Food to Allow

The amounts given below are approximate quantities to allow per head per meal and can be used as a guide when catering for a number of people.

Meat

With bone	2 - 4 oz.
For made up dishes ...	2 - 3 oz.

Fish

With much bone	6 oz.
For made up dishes ...	2 - 3 oz.

Vegetables, weight as purchased

Beans (broad)	8 oz.
Beans (runner)	6 oz.
Brussels sprouts	6 oz.
Cabbage	8 oz.
Carrots	4 oz.
Celery	1 large head serves 4 - 5 persons
Greens (spring)	8 oz.
Onions (as a vegetable) ...	6 oz.

Parsnips	6 oz.
Peas (green)	8 oz.
Potatoes	4 - 6 oz.
Spinach	8 oz.
Turnips	8 oz.

Puddings

Sponge and suet puddings	1½ oz. flour, etc.
Pastry (for pies and puddings)	1½ oz. flour, etc.
Milk puddings, moulds, jellies	¼ pint milk, etc.
Batter	1 oz. flour
Fruit (pies, puddings, stewed)	4 - 5 oz. fruit
Custard, as sauce	½ pint milk per 4 people

Cereals

Rice (for curry, etc.) ...	1 - 1½ oz.
Macaroni	1 - 1½ oz.

Sauces

Sauces and gravies - ...	⅛ pint

First Course or Hors-D'Oeuvre

Avocado pears

Cut the pears in half and remove the stone. Cover the pear halves with oil, vinegar and salt and pepper. Allow to stand for at least 30 minutes before serving.

Grapefruit

Choose firm, ripe grapefruit and wipe the skins. Cut into halves and take out all the pips and the core. Loosen the flesh from the skin and cut into small pieces, leaving them as if uncut in the skins. Sweeten to taste with castor sugar and if liked flavour with a little sherry. Serve in glass dishes, decorated with angelica or a maraschino cherry. If possible, leave in the refrigerator until required.

Smoked salmon

Serve thin slices with wedges of lemon and thin slices of brown bread and butter. Serve cayenne pepper separately.

Smoked trout

Buy the trout already smoked and remove the bones if possible. Serve with horseradish sauce, lemon, cayenne pepper and thin slices of brown bread and butter.

Melon

Serve very cold, with castor sugar and powdered ginger served separately. Canteloupe and honeydew melon should be cut in slices. Small or Charentais melons are cut in half horizontally. Allow half a small melon per person.

Prawn cocktail

you will need:

small lettuce heart	1 teaspoon chilli vinegar
½ pint picked prawns	(if available)
3 tablespoons mayonnaise	1 teaspoon tarragon
1 tablespoon tomato purée	vinegar
or tomato ketchup	good pinch salt and
lemon	cayenne pepper

1 Wash and dry the lettuce very well. Pick out the small leaves and tear into small pieces.
2 Arrange in cocktail glasses, and place the prawns on top.
3 Mix the mayonnaise with the tomato purée or ketchup. To obtain the purée, rub one large skinned tomato through a fine sieve.
4 Add the vinegars and salt and pepper to the mayonnaise mixture.

5 Pour this mixture over the prawns and garnish each 'cocktail' with a piece of lemon and a dusting of cayenne pepper. Serve very cold.

Ham and pineapple salad

you will need:

8 oz. ham, cooked	mayonnaise
1 small fresh pineapple or	gherkins
1 small can pineapple	

1 Cut the ham into short strips.
2 Peel and core the pineapple (or drain the canned pineapple) and cut into small dice.
3 Toss lightly with mayonnaise. Place in a salad bowl and garnish with thin slices of gherkin.

Fried scampi

you will need:

8 oz. fresh or frozen	Batter:
Dublin Bay prawns	2 oz. flour
(weight when peeled)	1 egg
fat for frying	scant ¼ pint milk
tartare sauce	salt and pepper
lemon wedges	

1 Separate the frozen prawns or dry the fresh ones.
2 Make the batter by sifting the flour into a bowl and adding the egg and milk gradually. Beat until a smooth thick batter and season well.
3 Dip each prawn into batter and lower gently into very hot fat.
4 Cook quickly until golden brown and drain on crumpled kitchen paper.
5 Serve on a hot dish accompanied by tartare sauce and lemon wedges.

Potted shrimps

you will need:

1 pint shrimps (weight	little grated nutmeg
when picked)	lettuce
2 – 3 oz. butter	lemon
good pinch cayenne pepper	
pinch salt	

1 Heat the butter in a small pan and turn the shrimps over in it until they are well coated but not cooked.
2 Add the seasonings and the nutmeg, mix well and pour into small moulds or dishes.
3 Leave until the butter has set.
4 Turn out on to a plate lined with crisp lettuce and garnish with lemon.
5 Serve with cayenne pepper and crisp toast.

Chicken liver pâté

cooking time 15-20 minutes

you will need:

2 8–oz. packets quick frozen chicken livers	1½ teaspoons salt
6 oz. butter, softened	½ teaspoon grated nutmeg
2 teaspoons dry mustard	dash cayenne pepper

1 Allow the chicken livers to thaw.

2 When they are thawed place in a saucepan and cover with water. Cover and simmer for 15 or 20 minutes until tender.

3 Drain and press through a sieve.

4 Add the butter, mustard, salt, nutmeg and cayenne pepper and mix together thoroughly.

5 Keep the pâté covered in a refrigerator and allow to stand for 1 hour at room temperature to soften before serving.

If liked, 2 tablespoons very finely chopped onion may be cooked with the liver.

The pâté may be made a day before it is required.

Fish salad

you will need:

12 oz. cooked white fish	1 lettuce
seasoning	mayonnaise or salad cream
1 tablespoon lemon juice	tomatoes or cucumber
1 tablespoon chopped mint	lemon wedges
1 tablespoon chopped parsley	

1 Flake the fish into a bowl and season to taste with salt and pepper. Mix with the lemon juice, mint and parsley, reserving 1 mixed teaspoon mint and parsley for garnishing.

2 Shred the outside leaves of the lettuce and arrange on a salad plate. Pile the fish in the centre and completely cover with mayonnaise or salad cream. Sprinkle with the teaspoon mixed herbs.

3 Arrange the remaining lettuce and tomatoes or cucumber round the fish and garnish with lemon wedges.

Tuna coleslaw

you will need:

small white cabbage	seasoning
3 heaped tablespoons shredded or chopped pineapple	3 tomatoes
	1 small can anchovy fillets
2 tablespoons vinegar	2 7–oz. cans middle cut tuna
2 tablespoons salad oil	

1 Shred the cabbage as finely as possible.

2 Mix with the pineapple, vinegar, salad oil and a pinch of salt and pepper. This should be done 30 minutes before serving.

3 Arrange in a salad bowl, top with the tomatoes cut into wedges, the anchovy fillets in rolls and flaked tuna.

4 Serve with wafer thin slices of brown bread and butter.

Chicken salad Caprice

you will need:

8 or 12 oz. cooked chicken	3 tablespoons mayonnaise
1 large ripe banana	2 tablespoons cream
2 tablespoons lemon juice	4 oz. black grapes
1 large orange	crisp lettuce leaves

1 Slice the banana into a bowl and turn over and over in the lemon juice.

2 Peel the orange, removing all skin and pith and add the segments to the bowl.

3 Add the chicken, diced, the mayonnaise and the cream.

4 Mix together lightly and leave in a cool place for 1 hour.

5 To serve, line a shallow bowl with crisp lettuce leaves and pile the chicken salad in the centre.

6 Garnish with halved, seeded grapes.

Tomato soup

cooking time about 1½ hours

you will need:

1 lb. fresh or canned tomatoes	lemon juice
	cornflour
1 onion	bunch herbs
1 carrot	salt and pepper
½ oz. butter	sugar
1 oz. bacon scraps	¼ pint double cream
1 pint white stock or juice from canned tomatoes	chopped chives
grated nutmeg	

1 Slice the tomatoes, onion and carrot. If canned tomatoes are used, strain them and make the juice up to 1 pint with stock.

2 Melt the butter in a deep pan and lightly fry the sliced vegetables and bacon (chopped) for 10 minutes.

3 Boil the stock or tomato juice and add to the vegetables with the nutmeg, lemon juice and herb, cook 45 minutes - 1 hour until tender.

4 Press through a nylon sieve using a wooden spoon. Measure purée and thicken, allowing ½ oz. cornflour blended with a little cold milk to each pint.

5 Stir in blended cornflour, bring slowly to the boil, stirring. Allow to cook for 2 - 3 minutes.

6 Season to taste with salt, pepper and a little sugar.

7 To serve, whip the cream, swirl on top of the soup, sprinkle with chopped chives.

Quick cream of chicken soup

cooking time 20 - 25 minutes

you will need:

1 oz. butter	salt and pepper
1 oz. flour	nutmeg
½ pint chicken stock	4 – 6 oz. cooked chicken
¼ pint milk	2 tablespoons cream

1 Melt the butter and stir in the flour, cook over a gentle heat for 3 minutes.
2 Gradually add stock, then milk, stirring well throughout, bring to the boil.
3 Season with salt, pepper and a little freshly grated nutmeg, add chicken, minced or chopped, and cook gently for 10 - 15 minutes.
4 Stir in cream and serve.

Watercress and potato soup

cooking time about 40 minutes

you will need:

1 lb. potatoes	4 oz. watercress
1 onion	salt and cayenne pepper
1 oz. butter	$\frac{1}{2}$ pint milk
$\frac{3}{4}$ pint stock	$\frac{1}{8}$ pint cream

1 Peel and chop the potatoes. Chop the onion finely.
2 Melt the butter and gently fry the vegetables without colouring.
3 Bring the stock to the boil, plunge in the watercress (previously washed) remove and chop finely.
4 Pour the stock and milk over the potatoes and simmer until tender.
5 Sieve potatoes, add the watercress, and bring back to the boil.
6 Reduce heat and stir in the cream, do not allow to boil.
7 Season to taste with salt and cayenne pepper and serve garnished with small sprigs of watercress.

Fish Dishes

Halibut and hollandaise sauce

cooking time 30 - 35 minutes

you will need:

4 halibut steaks	2 egg yolks
2 tablespoons white wine	4 oz. butter
2 tablespoons milk	salt
2 oz. luxury margarine	cayenne pepper
hollandaise sauce:	*Potato border:*
juice $\frac{1}{2}$ lemon	1-1$\frac{1}{2}$ lb. cooked potatoes
1 teaspoon water	2 oz. soft margarine
	seasoning

1 Clean the fish and remove the black skin. Place in an ovenproof dish with the wine, milk and margarine.
2 Cover with foil or greaseproof paper and bake on the middle shelf of a moderately hot oven (375° F.—Mark 5).

3 Meanwhile, make the sauce. Place the lemon juice, water and egg yolks in a bowl and stand over a saucepan of hot water.
4 Add a little of the butter and whisk until the mixture thickens.
5 Remove from the heat, gradually add the remaining butter. Season to taste and keep warm.
6 Rub the potatoes through a sieve. Heat in a saucepan with the margarine and beat until creamy. Season to taste.
7 Pipe the potato round the edge of an oven-proof serving dish. Brown under the grill or in the oven. Place the fish in the centre and pour on a little of the liquid in which it was cooked.
8 Decorate with chopped parsley and quarters of peeled orange.
9 Serve at once with the hollandaise sauce.

Halibut and orange salad

cooking time 10 - 15 minutes

you will need:

4 – 6 oz. halibut fillets	mayonnaise
salt and pepper	1 bunch watercress
1 lettuce	2 oranges

1 Prepare the fillets, season and fold in half.
2 Steam for 10 - 15 minutes, between two plates. Allow to become cool.
3 Wash the lettuce and shred the outer leaves and place on a dish.
4 Place the fillets on top of this. Coat each evenly with mayonnaise.
5 Garnish with the remaining lettuce and sprigs of watercress.
6 Slice the oranges, having removed the skin, and arrange round the dish.

Haddock in cream

cooking time 30 - 40 minutes

you will need:

4 fillets or cutlets of haddock	salt and pepper
	3 small onions
2 tablespoons lemon juice	$\frac{1}{4}$ pint single cream
$\frac{1}{2}$ teaspoon Worcestershire sauce	

1 Slice the onions and place in a greased oven-proof dish.
2 Place the fish on top, sprinkle with salt and pepper, lemon juice and Worcestershire sauce.
3 Pour on the cream and bake in a moderate oven (350° F.—Mark 4) with a lid on.

Baked haddock suprême

cooking time 15 - 20 minutes

you will need:

4 fillets fresh haddock	1 head celery
salt and pepper	1 15-oz. can whole peeled
1 medium sized onion	tomatoes
(finely chopped)	1 small green pepper
4 tablespoons dry white	parsley
wine	

1 Wipe the fillets and season lightly to taste.
2 Place on a large plate, sprinkle with the finely chopped onion and the wine. Leave for 1 - 2 hours.
3 Wash the celery and cut into 1-inch lengths. Place in the bottom of a fireproof dish.
4 Arrange the fish on top. Add any remaining onion and wine.
5 Strain the tomatoes and place round the fish in a moderately hot oven (375° F.—Mark 5).
6 Garnish with very fine rings of pepper and parsley.

Lemon fish casserole

cooking time about 35 minutes

you will need:

1½ - 2 lbs. cod cutlets	pinch ground ginger
1 large onion	2 eggs
1 oz. butter	juice 1 lemon
pinch cayenne pepper	1 oz. flour
salt	

1 Melt the butter and fry the sliced onion until soft.
2 Place the washed fish in a casserole and pour the onion and butter over it.
3 Sprinkle with salt, pepper and ginger and add 3 tablespoons water. Cover and cook in a moderate oven (350° F.—Mark 4) for about 25 minutes.
4 Blend the beaten eggs, flour and lemon juice together.
5 Add a little liquid from the fish, mix thoroughly and pour over the fish. Continue cooking uncovered for a further 10 minutes.
6 Serve the fish from the casserole accompanied by baked tomatoes and creamed potatoes.

Escallops with rice

cooking time about 15 minutes

you will need:

4 large escallops	8 rashers streaky bacon
6 oz. Patna rice	4 slices pineapple

1 Boil the rice in fast boiling salted water until just cooked.

2 Meanwhile, wash the escallops, trim away the beard and any black parts. Cut each in half.
3 Roll each half in a rasher of bacon and thread on a skewer with half a ring of pineapple between each.
4 Grill under a moderate heat for 8 - 10 minutes, turning once.
5 Drain the rice, rinse under running cold water, then reheat.
6 Pile the rice on a dish and lay the skewers on top. Serve at once.

Poached salmon trout

you will need:

salmon trout	salt
water	

1 Clean the fish, removing the gills, intestines and eyes but leaving on the head and tail.
2 Place the fish in a piece of muslin and lower into simmering salted water (1 teaspoon salt to every 2 pints water). If a fish kettle is not available, a large saucepan can be used.
3 Poach the fish until it is cooked, allowing 10 minutes per pound and 10 minutes over.
4 When the fish is cooked, lift carefully from the water and drain.
5 When serving hot, place on a flat dish and garnish with sliced cucumber, chopped parsley and lemon slices. Serve accompanied by new potatoes and hollandaise sauce or melted butter.
6 When serving cold, serve plain, accompanied by mayonnaise and salad.

Fillets of sole bonne femme

cooking time 10 - 15 minutes

you will need:

4 fillets of sole	seasoning
4 oz. mushrooms	¼ pint white wine
1 shallot	¼ pint white sauce
1 teaspoon chopped	(see page 59)
parsley	butter

1 Wipe the fillets with a damp cloth, place in a pan with the sliced mushrooms, shallot, parsley and salt and pepper to taste.
2 Cover with the wine and poach gently until cooked.
3 When cooked, remove the fish and keep warm. Boil the wine quickly until it is reduced by half.
4 Stir the reduced wine into the hot white sauce and add a little butter. Stir until thoroughly blended and pour at once over the fillets.
5 Place under the grill until golden brown. Serve at once.

Plaice mornay

cooking time 30 minutes

you will need:

4 4 oz. fillets of plaice	salt and pepper
½ pint white sauce (see page 59)	mustard
	grated nutmeg
2 tablespoons grated cheese	

1 Wash the fish, fold the fillets in half and steam between two plates.
2 Season the sauce to taste with salt, pepper and a little mustard.
3 Add the cheese, reserving a little, and a little grated nutmeg.
4 Arrange the cooked fish in a shallow fireproof dish. Coat with the sauce and sprinkle on the remaining cheese.
5 Place under a hot grill or in a moderate oven until golden brown.

Poached salmon

you will need:

salmon (allow 4 – 6 oz. per person)	½ leek
	1 strip celery
To every 2 pints water use:	6 peppercorns
1 dessertspoon salt	*bouquet garni*
1 small turnip	
1 small onion	

1 Use only enough water to cover the fish. Place in a pan and bring to the boil.
2 Prepare the vegetables and add to the water with the salt and simmer for 30 minutes.
3 Meanwhile, wash, clean and scale the fish and tie loosely in muslin.
4 Remove any scum from the pan and add the fish. Boil gently until the salmon is cooked, allowing 10 minutes per pound for a thick piece and 7 minutes per pound for a tail piece.
5 When cooked, drain carefully, place on a dish and garnish with parsley.
6 Serve with sliced cucumber and hollandaise sauce.

Salmon mayonnaise

you will need:

cold boiled or poached salmon	beetroot
	gherkins
lettuce	capers
mayonnaise	anchovy fillets
cucumber	hard–boiled eggs

1 Wash the lettuce, shred it and place in the bottom of a salad bowl.
2 Remove the skin and bone from the salmon and flake roughly. Arrange on the lettuce.
3 Completely cover the salmon with mayonnaise.
4 Garnish with sliced cucumber and beetroot and decorate with sliced gherkins, capers, anchovy fillets and hard-boiled egg.

Lobster mayonnaise

you will need:

1 boiled lobster	salad
mayonnaise	

1 Cut the lobster in half lengthways.
2 Scoop out the meat from the body, mix it with a little mayonnaise and return it to the body.
3 Remove the meat from the tail carefully and slice it. Arrange it in the shell in overlapping slices with the red part uppermost.
4 Serve the lobster on a plate of salad and garnish with the claws. Serve mayonnaise separately.

Dressed crab

you will need:

1 crab (2½ – 3 lb.)	French dressing
seasoning	1 hard–boiled egg
fresh breadcrumbs	parsley (chopped)
lemon juice (optional)	

1 Pick the crab meat from the shells keeping the dark meat separate from the white.
2 Mix the dark meat with salt and pepper to taste, breadcrumbs and a little lemon juice if liked.
3 Press the mixture lightly round the sides of the well washed shell.
4 Flake the white meat in a small bowl and mix with French dressing. Pile into the centre of the shell.
5 Sieve the egg yolk and chop the white.
6 Garnish the crab with the egg and parsley and decorate with the small claws. Place on a flat dish and surround with salad.

Baked crab ramekins

cooking time 30 - 35 minutes

you will need:

1 packet frozen spinach	1 carton sour cream
4 oz. cheese, grated	½ level teaspoon salt
12 oz. flaked fresh or canned crab meat	dash pepper
	dash nutmeg
1 dessertspoon lemon juice	1 tablespoon sherry
2 teaspoons finely chopped onion	8 oz. can whole peeled tomatoes

1 Cook the spinach according to the directions on the packet. Drain well.
2 Spread in 4 greased ramekin or individual baking dishes.
3 Sprinkle each with a little cheese.
4 Divide the crab meat between the 4 dishes and sprinkle each with lemon juice.
5 Blend the onion, sour cream, salt, pepper, nutmeg and sherry together and pour over the crab.
6 Top each with strained tomato and the rest of the cheese.
7 Bake uncovered at 350° F.—Mark 4.

Meat and Poultry Dishes

Spiced beef and tomato casserole
cooking time 1½ - 2 hours

you will need:

1 lb. stewing steak	½ pint water
¾ oz. flour	¼ pint red wine
1 level teaspoon curry powder	1 dessertspoon vinegar
	1 onion (sliced)
2 tablespoons corn oil	3 carrots (chopped)
1 packet tomato sauce mix	2 sticks celery (chopped)
1 beef stock cube	1 green pepper (chopped)
2 level dessertspoons brown sugar	

1 Mix the flour and curry powder together.
2 Cut the meat into cubes and toss in the flour.
3 Heat the corn oil and sauté the meat in it for a few minutes.
4 Add the tomato sauce mix, crumbled stock cube, sugar, water, wine, vinegar, onion, carrots, celery and the pepper.
5 Bring slowly to boiling point, stirring all the time. Transfer to a casserole.
6 Cover and cook in a slow oven at 310° F.—Mark 2.

Lamb chops and mushrooms
cooking time about 40 minutes

you will need:

4 lamb chops	1 oz. flour
1 oz. butter	½ pint brown stock
8 oz. mushrooms	seasoning

1 Melt the butter in a frying pan and fry the prepared chops and mushrooms, removing as they are cooked—about 20 minutes.
2 When all are cooked, stir in the flour and cook until brown.
3 Add the stock and season to taste with salt and pepper.
4 Return the chops and mushrooms to the pan and reheat gently for about 15 minutes.
5 Serve accompanied by creamed potato and peas.

Creamed chicken à la king
cooking time about 30 minutes

you will need:

12 oz. cooked chicken, diced	1 oz. flour
3 oz. red or green pepper	1 level teaspoon salt
1 oz. butter	½ pint chicken stock
1 dessertspoon finely chopped onion	1 dessertspoon lemon juice
4 oz. button mushrooms, sliced	2 egg yolks
	¼ pint thin cream

1 Blanch the pepper, remove the seeds and chop finely.
2 Melt the butter in a saucepan, stir in the pepper, onion and mushrooms. Cook over a gentle heat until soft.

3 Add the flour and salt and cook for a further 2 - 3 minutes, stirring.
4 Stir in the chicken stock and lemon juice and bring to the boil, stirring all the time. Add the chicken and heat through without boiling.
5 Beat the egg yolks and cream together and thin with a little liquid from the pan. Stir into the chicken mixture and cook very gently for a few minutes until thick and creamy. Do not allow to boil.
6 Serve with crisp toast.

Grilled chicken with almonds
cooking time about 25 minutes

you will need:

4 chicken quarters	1 tablespoon lemon juice
salt	*Garnish:*
2½ oz. butter	small bunch watercress
2 oz. blanched shredded almonds	lemon quarters

1 Season the joints with salt.
2 Melt the butter in the grill pan (having removed the rack) and turn the joints in it, until evenly coated with butter.
3 Arrange chicken skin side down and grill steadily under a medium grill for about 8 - 10 minutes.
4 Turn the joints over, baste with butter and continue grilling for another 10 - 15 minutes.
5 Arrange the joints on a hot serving dish and keep hot.
6 Put the almonds into the grill pan and grill, turning, until golden brown. Stir in the lemon juice.
7 Pour over the chicken joints and just before serving, garnish with watercress and lemon quarters.

Casserole of veal
cooking time about 1½ hours

you will need:

1½ lb. lean stewing veal	¼ pint thin cream
1 pint thick white sauce (see page 59)	2 teaspoons lemon juice
	bacon rolls
2 dozen button mushrooms	lemon slices
seasoning	

1 Wipe the meat, trimming off any skin or fat.
2 Cut into small pieces and place in a casserole. Bring the sauce to the boil, add the mushrooms and season to taste with salt and pepper.
3 Stand the casserole in a pan of water and cook in a moderate oven (350° F.—Mark 4).
4 When cooked, stir in the cream and lemon juice, top with grilled bacon rolls. Garnish with slices of lemon and serve at once in the casserole.

Austrian steak

cooking time about 15 minutes

you will need for each person:

4 oz. rump steak, cut very thinly	horseradish sauce watercress
2 large mushrooms	potato crisps
1 oz. butter	

1 Melt the butter in a frying pan.
2 When it begins to brown, add the steak, brown on both sides and then cook to the tenderness required (5-10 minutes).
3 When the steak is nearly cooked, add the mushrooms.
4 Remove the steak to a warm dish and garnish with mushrooms, placing a little horseradish sauce in each.
5 Serve with potato crisps and watercress.
If liked, 2 - 3 tablespoons wine can be added to the pan. Bring to the boil and pour over the steak.

Wiener schnitzel

cooking time 10 minutes

you will need:

4 veal escalopes	capers
seasoned flour	anchovy fillets
egg and browned breadcrumbs	lemon slices
oil or butter for frying	sprigs parsley

1 Beat the veal with a rolling pin until thin.
2 Toss each escalope in a little seasoned flour, shaking off surplus flour, but making sure they are well coated.
3 Dip in beaten egg and then into breadcrumbs. Shake to remove any surplus crumbs.
4 Fry in melted butter or oil for about 5 minutes on each side until golden brown.
5 Drain on crumpled absorbent paper.
6 Arrange the escalopes on a hot serving dish and garnish with capers, drained anchovy fillets, lemon slices and sprigs of parsley. Serve at once accompanied by sauté potatoes.

Beef Strogonoff

cooking time 2 - 3 hours

you will need:

2 lb. stewing beef	½ pint stock
2 small onions	1 teaspoon salt
1 carton sour cream	½ teaspoon pepper
4 oz. mushrooms	pinch mustard
4 oz. butter	1 glass red wine
1 tablespoon tomato purée	nutmeg

1 Cut the beef into cubes. Sprinkle with salt, pepper and mustard.
2 Chop the onions and slice the mushrooms.
3 Melt the butter and fry the onions and mushrooms for about 2 minutes. Add the beef and fry for 5 minutes.

4 Stir in the tomato purée, wine and stock. Bring to the boil, cover, and simmer over a gentle heat.
5 Add the sour cream during the last 30 minutes of cooking.
6 Re-season if necessary and serve sprinkled with nutmeg accompanied by creamed potatoes and small whole carrots.

Steak and kidney pie

cooking time about 2 hours

you will need:

2 oz. sheep's or 6 oz. ox kidneys	stock or water
1½ lb. lean steak	8 oz. flaky pastry (see page 69)
seasoned flour	beaten egg
2 onions	

1 Soak the kidneys. Remove the skin and core and cut into slices.
2 Wipe the steak, cut into cubes and toss in seasoned flour, with the kidneys.
3 Peel and finely chop the onions.
4 Fill a pie dish with the meat and onions, add enough stock or water to quarter fill the dish.
5 Cover and cook in a slow oven until tender. Allow to cool.
6 Roll the pastry out and use to cover the pie. Brush with egg.
7 Make a small hole in the centre of the pie.
8 Bake in a hot oven (450° F.—Mark 8) on the middle shelf for 30 minutes.

Stuffed breast of veal

cooking time about 1½ hours

you will need:

1 boned breast of veal (about 2 lb.)	bouquet garni
12 oz. sausage meat	6 peppercorns
1 large onion	salt
1 carrot	pepper
½ turnip	8 oz. Patna rice
	2 oz. grated cheese

1 Season the veal with salt and pepper, spread the sausage meat over the inner surface, roll up and tie securely with string.
2 Slice the onion, carrot and turnip, and place with peppercorns and bouquet garni in a large pan. Add ½ pint water.
3 Place the rolled veal on top, cover with foil and a lid.
4 Cook gently, basting occasionally and adding more water if necessary.
5 Cook the rice in about 1½ pints stock or water for 10-15 minutes. Drain. Stir in the grated cheese and season to taste.
6 Serve the veal cut in slices and arranged down the centre of a hot dish, surrounded by the rice. Accompany by a green salad.

Western style chops

cooking time 35 - 40 minutes

you will need:

4 chops, cut ¼ inch thick from short back bacon	1 can sweet corn kernels
1 medium onion, chopped	1 level teaspoon flour
1 15-oz. can whole peeled tomatoes	¼ level teaspoon sage seasoning

1 Remove the rind from the chops and snip the fat at 1-inch intervals. This will prevent curling.
2 Brown quickly on both sides in a frying pan, remove and keep warm.
3 Add the onion to the pan and cook for 3 - 4 minutes.
4 Place in the bottom of a large casserole.
5 Add the strained tomatoes, then the chops and cover with the sweet corn.
6 Blend the tomato juice with the cornflour and sage and pour over the ingredients in the casserole. Season to taste.
7 Cover and bake at 375° F.—Mark 5—until the chops are tender.
8 Serve with baked potatoes and a green salad.

Stuffed loin of pork

you will need:

2½ – 3 lb. loin of pork, boned	1 level tablespoon chopped onion
salt and pepper	
little dripping	2 oz. lean streaky bacon, chopped
Stuffing:	
4 oz. breadcrumbs	1 hard-boiled egg, chopped
2 level tablespoons chopped parsley	8 oz. can whole peeled tomatoes (strained)
salt and pepper	

1 Place all the stuffing ingredients in a bowl and mix thoroughly, seasoning to taste.
2 Season the pork and spread with stuffing.
3 Roll up and tie securely with string.
4 Place in a roasting tin with a little dripping and roast at 425° F.—Mark 7—allowing 25 minutes per pound and 25 minutes over.
If there is any stuffing left over, it may be shaped into balls and placed round the joint 30 minutes before the end of cooking time.

Veal with tomatoes and spaghetti

cooking time 25 - 30 minutes

you will need:

4 veal escalopes	1 small green pepper, chopped
egg and breadcrumbs	
1 oz. butter	1 15-oz. can whole peeled tomatoes
1 small onion, chopped	
4 oz. mushrooms, sliced	butter for frying
6 oz. spaghetti	

1 Dip the meat in egg and breadcrumbs.
2 Melt the 1 oz. butter and fry the onion without browning for 4 - 5 minutes.
3 Add the mushrooms and pepper and cook a further 5 minutes.
4 Add the tomatoes, strained and heat through.
5 Fry the veal in butter for 4 - 5 minutes on each side.
6 Meanwhile, cook the spaghetti in plenty of fast boiling salted water for 10 - 12 minutes. Drain well and toss in a little butter.
7 Serve the veal with the spaghetti and vegetable.

Vegetables and Salads

French mashed potatoes

cooking time 25 - 30 minutes

you will need:

2 lb. potatoes	seasoning
1 oz. butter or margarine	chopped parsley
milk	

1 Peel the potatoes and slice them. Place in a saucepan.
2 Add the butter or margarine and cover with cold milk.
3 Cook very gently over a low heat.
4 When tender, mash them in the saucepan, seasoning with salt and pepper. Beat thoroughly.
5 Turn into a hot serving dish and sprinkle with chopped parsley.

Potato straws

Proceed as for potato chips, cutting the potatoes into straws about the size of a matchstick. Lower into hot fat and fry for 1 minute. Reheat the fat and fry the straws for about 2 minutes until crisp and brown. Drain on crumpled absorbent paper, sprinkle with salt and serve at once.

Duchess potatoes

cooking time 30 minutes

you will need:

1 lb. potatoes	1 egg
1 oz. butter or margarine	seasoning
cream or top of milk	grated nutmeg

1 Peel the potatoes and boil until tender in salted water.
2 Put through a sieve and mix with the butter or margarine, beaten egg and enough cream or top of the milk to give a smooth mixture that will stand in peaks. Season with salt, pepper and grated nutmeg.
3 Pipe through a star-shaped nozzle on to a greased baking tray in rounds. Glaze carefully with a little beaten egg.
4 Bake in a hot oven until crisp and brown.

Sauté potatoes

Boil 6 medium-sized potatoes in their skins until they are just soft. Let them dry thoroughly, then peel and slice them ¼ inch thick. Heat 1 - 2 oz. butter or margarine in a frying pan, add the potatoes, sprinkle with salt and pepper and toss in the hot fat until lightly browned. Serve at once.

Baked potatoes in their jackets

cooking time about 1½ hours

you will need:

4 large potatoes	butter or margarine

1 Scrub the potatoes, wash and dry them.
2 Brush with melted butter or margarine or rub with a greasy butter or margarine paper. Prick each with a fork.
3 Bake on the shelves of a hot oven (400° F.—Mark 6).
4 Turn the potatoes over once or twice whilst they are cooking.
5 Cut a cross in the top of each potato when cooked and insert a piece of butter. Serve at once.

Potato croquettes

you will need:

1 lb. cooked potatoes	egg and breadcrumbs
1 oz. butter or margarine	deep fat
1 egg	1 teaspoon chopped
salt and pepper	parsley or 2 tablespoons
	grated cheese (optional)

1 Put the potatoes through a sieve and cream in a saucepan with the butter or margarine, beaten egg and seasoning to taste. If liked, add parsley or grated cheese.
2 Form the potato mixture into small rolls or balls. Coat each twice with egg and breadcrumbs.
3 Fry in hot deep fat for about 5 minutes until brown. Drain and serve.

Potato chips

Scrub and peel even sized potatoes thinly. Cut into lengths about 2 inches long and ½ inch wide and thick. Place them into cold water as soon as they are cut. Rinse and drain them and dry in a clean cloth. Put into a frying basket and lower into hot deep fat (360°). Cook until the potatoes are soft, but not brown, about 3 minutes. Lift out the basket and reheat the fat to 375°. Place the basket back into the fat and fry until the potatoes are crisp and brown, about another 3 minutes. Drain on crumpled absorbent paper, sprinkle with salt and serve at once.

Boiled asparagus

cooking time 15 - 20 minutes

you will need:

1 bundle asparagus	2 oz. butter, melted
salt	lemon juice

1 Trim the hard white ends of the asparagus to suitable lengths for serving.
2 Working from the heads downwards scrape the stalks with a sharp knife and wash well in cold water.
3 Tie into small bundles keeping the heads all at one end.
4 Cut the stalks evenly. Stand in cold water until ready to cook.
5 Cook very gently in just enough boiling salted water to cover, making sure the heads are away from the direct heat.
6 When the asparagus is tender, drain carefully and serve on a folded table napkin, accompanied by the butter, lightly salted and flavoured with lemon juice.

Baked mushrooms

cooking time 25-30 minutes

you will need:

18–24 flat mushrooms	powdered mace
seasoning	butter or margarine

1 Wash the mushrooms under running water, peel the caps and trim the stalks.
2 Place mushrooms in a baking dish stalk side uppermost.
3 Sprinkle with salt and pepper and a little mace. Dot each with a tiny piece of butter or margarine.
4 Cover and cook in a moderate oven (350° F.—Mark 4).
5 Serve the mushrooms with their juice.

Mixed vegetables

conservatively cooked

you will need:

1 lb. mixed vegetables, using those that are in season	½ – 1 teacup boiling water salt and pepper chopped parsley
1 oz. butter or margarine	

1 Prepare the vegetables, cutting large ones into thin slices and halving the slices if necessary. If using young summer vegetables and they are really small, leave them whole.
2 Melt the butter or margarine in a saucepan.
3 Add the vegetables and toss in the hot fat, starting with those that take the longest to cook. If using tomatoes do not add until 5 minutes before serving.
4 Add the boiling water, using very little with summer vegetables.
5 Simmer gently until all the vegetables are tender.
6 Season and serve hot sprinkled with chopped parsley.

Boiled spinach

you will need:

3 lb. spinach	2 tablespoons cream
1 oz. butter	(optional)
salt and pepper	

1 Pick the spinach over carefully and wash in at least 3 changes of cold water. Break off the stalks, pulling out the centre ribs if they are tough.
2 Place the wet leaves in a saucepan, pressing well down. Do not add any water.
3 Cook gently for about 15 minutes until tender, stirring occasionally.
4 Drain well, pressing out all the water.
5 Reheat the spinach in the butter, adding the cream if used. Mix well and season to taste with salt and pepper.

Glazed carrots

cooking time about 45 minutes

you will need:

1½ lb. young carrots	¼ teaspoon salt
2 oz. butter	stock
3 lumps sugar	chopped parsley

1 Scrape the carrots, leaving them whole.
2 Melt the butter, add the carrots, sugar, salt and enough stock to come half way up the carrots.
3 Cook gently without a lid until tender, giving the pan an occasional shake.
4 When tender, remove the carrots and keep hot. Boil the remaining liquid until it is reduced to a glaze.
5 Add the carrots to the glaze two or three at a time and turn them until they are well coated with glaze.
6 Turn into a hot serving dish and sprinkle with chopped parsley.

Peas Parisian

cooking time about 1 hour

you will need:

1½ pints shelled peas	2 teaspoons sugar
4 tiny onions or spring	salt and pepper
onions	egg yolk (optional)
1 lettuce	
2 oz. butter	

1 Peel the onions.
2 Remove the outer leaves of the lettuce and wash the heart, leaving it whole.
3 Place the peas in a thick saucepan with the lettuce heart, onions, the butter cut into small pieces. Stir in the sugar and season lightly with salt and pepper.
4 Cover with a lid and cook gently over a low heat shaking the pan occasionally.
5 Re-season if liked and serve.
6 If liked the liquid in the pan may be thickened with an egg yolk before serving.

Steamed cucumbers

cooking time 25 - 30 minutes

you will need:

2 cucumbers	lemon juice
¼ pint white sauce (see	fresh tarragon leaves
page 59) or hollandaise	(if available)
sauce (see page 51)	

1 Wash the cucumbers, but do not peel them.
2 Steam them whole until tender, then drain and cut them into 2-inch lengths.
3 Stand the lengths upright in a hot dish and coat with the hot white sauce, flavoured with a little lemon juice.
4 Garnish with a little finely-chopped tarragon leaves if possible.

Pineapple salad

you will need:

1 small pineapple	mayonnaise
1 celery heart	lemon slices

1 Peel and core the pineapple and cut into fine shreds.
2 Wash the celery, cut into shreds and mix with the pineapple. Mix with just enough mayonnaise to moisten.
3 Serve very cold, garnished with thin slices of lemon.

Beetroot salad

you will need:

2 small cooked beetroots	grated horseradish
French dressing	

1 Dice the beetroot and place in a bowl.
2 Sprinkle with freshly grated horseradish and pour on a little French dressing. Turn over once or twice and serve.

Chicory with white sauce

cooking time 30 - 40 minutes

you will need:

4 large heads chicory	salt
½ pint white sauce	lemon juice
(see page 59)	

1 Cut the hard end off the chicory and remove the outer leaves.
2 Split each head to within ½ inch of the end and wash well in cold water.
3 Place the chicory in a pan, just cover with water. Bring to the boil and cook for 5 minutes.
4 Drain, tie the chicory together in bundles of two and cook gently in boiling salted water until tender.
5 Add lemon juice to taste to the hot, well-seasoned sauce.
6 Drain the chicory, remove the string and place in a hot serving dish. Pour the sauce over the chicory and serve at once.

Pears with nut and date salad

you will need:

3 ripe dessert pears	2 oz. chopped walnuts
lemon juice	parsley
1 crisp lettuce	French or salad dressing
4 oz. chopped dates	

1 Peel and halve the pears, remove the cores and a little of the pear flesh, to leave a hollow. Sprinkle the pears with lemon juice to keep the colour.
2 Wash the lettuce and shred a few of the leaves, lining a salad plate with the remainder. If preferred, individual plates can be used.
3 Place the shredded lettuce, dates, walnuts, the chopped pear flesh and a little chopped parsley in a bowl. Mix lightly together with French dressing or salad dressing.
4 Divide this mixture between the pear halves, piling it up in the prepared hollow. Place the pears on the lettuce and serve.
If fresh pears are not available, canned pears, well drained, can be used.

Celery and nut salad

you will need:

2 cooking apples or oranges	
4 oz. grapes	crisp lettuce leaves, cos
1 large or 2 small celery hearts	if possible
	walnut halves
mayonnaise or salad dressing	

1 Quarter the apples, core them and cut into thin slices, or remove the skin and pith from the oranges and quarter.
2 Halve the grapes and remove the pips. Wash the celery and cut into shreds.

3 Mix all together lightly with mayonaise or salad dressing.
4 Line a plate with crisp, well-washed lettuce leaves, pile the salad in the centre and garnish with the walnut halves.

Spanish salad

you will need:

1 large Spanish onion	French dressing
1 cucumber	2 tablespoons grated
6 tomatoes	Parmesan cheese
seasoning	6 stoned olives

1 Slice the onion very thinly.
2 Cut the cucumber into thin slices and the tomatoes into thicker slices.
3 Arrange in a bowl in layers, seasoning each layer with salt and pepper and sprinkling with French dressing and the grated cheese.
4 Garnish with olives.

Potato salad

you will need:

6 large new potatoes	1 tablespoon chopped parsley
$\frac{1}{2}$ pint salad dressing	seasoning
2 finely chopped spring onions or 1 heaped tea-spoon chopped chives	tomatoes or radishes cress

1 Boil the potatoes in their jackets until they are just soft.
2 While they are hot, peel and cut into neat dice, and mix with the dressing, spring onions or chives, parsley, salt and pepper to taste.
3 Pile on to a dish and garnish with overlapping slices of radish or tomato and cress.

Sauces and Dressings

White sauce

cooking time about 10 minutes
you will need:

1 oz. butter	$\frac{1}{2}$ pint milk
1 oz. flour	seasoning

1 Melt the butter and stir in the flour using a wooden spoon.
2 Cook over a gentle heat for 3 minutes without browning, stirring throughout.
3 Remove from heat and gradually stir in half the milk, stir hard until well blended.
4 Return to heat, cook slowly until sauce thickens, stirring.
5 Gradually add remaining liquid.
6 Bring to boil, season with salt and pepper.

Allow to boil for 2 - 3 minutes, stirring throughout.
This is a thick or coating sauce, used for cauliflower cheese, filling flans and baked casserole dishes.
For a thin or pouring sauce, use $\frac{1}{2}$ oz. butter and $\frac{1}{2}$ oz. flour. The amount of milk and method are the same.

Cheese sauce

To $\frac{1}{2}$ pint white sauce add 2 heaped table-spoons grated cheese, a little made mustard, a little salt and a pinch of cayenne pepper. Add the cheese when the sauce is at boiling point, mix well in but do not allow the sauce to boil again.

Mushroom sauce

Cook 2 - 4 oz. sliced mushrooms in 1 oz. butter very gently for about 15 minutes. Stir the mushrooms, butter and the juice into ½ pint hot white sauce. Season to taste.

Onion sauce

To ½ pint white sauce (made from half milk and half liquid in which the onions were cooked) add 2 chopped, boiled onions and a few drops of lemon juice.

Parsley sauce

To ½ pint boiling white sauce, add 1 heaped tablespoon chopped parsley and a squeeze of lemon juice if liked. Whisk in 1 oz. butter, a little piece at a time at just below boiling point.

French dressing

you will need:

1 tablespoon oil	⅛ teaspoon salt
pinch pepper	½ tablespoon malt or wine
pinch dry mustard	vinegar

1 Mix the oil and seasoning, stir in the vinegar, drop by drop.
2 Stir before using as the ingredients separate out.

Mayonnaise

you will need:

1 – 2 egg yolks (from fresh eggs)	vinegars to taste: 4 parts wine vinegar (or lemon juice), 2 parts tarragon and 1 part chilli vinegar
salt, pepper and mustard	
¼ – ½ pint best olive oil	

1 Place the egg yolks in a thick basin. Add salt, pepper and mustard to taste.
2 Whisk until the seasonings are well mixed with the yolks.
3 Very gradually add the oil, drop by drop, whisking all the time.
4 When the mayonnaise begins to thicken the oil can be added in a thin stream but the whisking must be continued all the time.
5 When the mixture is really thick, add a few drops of vinegar or lemon juice. This will thin the mixture down again and then oil can be added as before. Continue this process until the whole amount of oil is added.
6 Cover the mayonnaise with a damp cloth and store in a cool place. To use after storing— whisk again and add a few drops of vinegar.
7 If the mayonnaise should curdle, add the curdled mixture very gradually to a fresh egg yolk, whisking all the time.

Cold tartare sauce

To ¼ pint mayonnaise add the following: 1 teaspoon each of chopped gherkins, olives, capers, parsley and chives. Add a little French mustard and thin to the required consistency with about 1 dessertspoon wine vinegar and a little dry white wine if liked.

Cooked mayonnaise

you will need:

1 teaspoon castor sugar	1 tablespoon salad oil
1 teaspoon salt	3 egg yolks
1 level teaspoon dry mustard	¼ pint vinegar
good pinch pepper	½ pint milk or single cream

1 Mix the sugar, salt, mustard and pepper together in a bowl.
2 Stir in the oil, then the beaten eggs.
3 Gradually add the vinegar and lastly the milk or cream.
4 Stand the bowl in a saucepan with enough boiling water to come half way up the side of the bowl.
5 Stir the mixture all the time until it thickens. Allow to become cold and re-season.
6 This salad dressing will keep well in a cool place.

Sour cream dressing

you will need:

sour, thick cream	little made mustard
seasoning	little castor sugar

1 Place the cream in a bowl and stir until smooth.
2 Season to taste with salt, pepper, mustard and sugar.
3 If the dressing is very thick, it can be thinned down with a little top of the milk.

Cream salad dressing

you will need:

1 saltspoon made mustard	1 tablespoon oil
1 saltspoon salt	1 dessertspoon vinegar (a
pepper	mixture of malt and
pinch castor sugar	tarragon)
2 tablespoons double cream	

1 Mix the mustard, salt, pepper to taste and castor sugar together. Stir in the cream.
2 Add the oil drop by drop, stirring all the time.
3 Add the vinegar slowly and stir well.

Sauce Tyrol
(To serve with roast chicken or veal)

Blend a 5 oz. carton cultured cream with 1 egg yolk. Add a pinch of pepper and salt and ¼ teaspoon made mustard. Stand in simmering water until warm. If liked, sliced olives or anchovy fillets can be added.

Herb cream

(To serve with hot vegetables: new potatoes, cauliflower, carrots, broccoli, spinach, celery)

Blend a 5 oz. carton cultured cream with 1 teaspoon chopped parsley, 1 teaspoon chopped chives (or garlic salt to taste), ½ teaspoon sweet basil, ¼ teaspoon thyme, sprinkling salt and white pepper.

Sharp sauce

(To serve with shrimp or lobster cocktails, egg salads, grilled or fried fish)

Blend a 5 oz. carton cultured cream with 3 tablespoons finely chopped onion, 1 tablespoon mayonnaise, 1 tablespoon capers or red pimento, ¼ teaspoon made mustard and a pinch of cayenne pepper. If liked, lemon juice can be added to taste.

Cucumber cream

(To serve with fish or chicken)

Blend a 5 oz. carton cultured cream with 1 tablespoon tarragon vinegar or lemon juice, 1 teaspoon chopped parsley or chervil, ¼ teaspoon salt. Peel and slice a medium-sized cucumber, sprinkle with salt, leave for 10 minutes, then drain. Place in a serving dish and top with cream. Dust the top with paprika pepper.

If cultured cream is not available, single cream with lemon juice can be used. To each ¼ pint single cream add 1 dessertspoon lemon juice. Stir and leave in a warm place for 10 minutes.

Party Desserts

Lemon meringue pie

cooking time 45 minutes

you will need:

7–inch baked pastry flan case	1 oz. butter
Filling:	*Meringue:*
1 oz. cornflour	2 egg whites
3 – 4 oz. sugar	pinch salt
2 egg yolks	4 oz. sugar
½ pint water	1 level teaspoon cornflour
2 large lemons	

1 Mix the cornflour, sugar and egg yolk smoothly with a little of the cold water.
2 Put the rest of the water on to heat with the thinly peeled lemon rind.

3 Strain on to the cornflour mixture, return to the pan and cook for 3 minutes, stirring throughout.
4 Remove from the heat, stir in the butter and the lemon juice. Turn into the baked pastry case. Bake in a moderate oven (350° F.—Mark 4) until set, about 30 minutes.
5 Beat the egg whites until stiff with the pinch of salt.
6 Mix the sugar and cornflour together. Fold lightly into the egg white.
7 Pile on top of the pie.
8 Place in a moderate oven (350° F.—Mark 4) for 10 - 15 minutes until golden.

Pineapple fritters

cooking time 3 - 4 minutes each

you will need:

4 oz. plain flour	2 cans small pineapple rings
pinch salt	
1 egg	fat for frying
¼ pint milk	cinnamon or ground ginger (optional)

1 Sift the flour and salt together. Make a well in the centre, add the egg and some of the milk. Mix until a stiff consistency using more milk as required. Beat thoroughly until smooth. Leave to stand for 30 minutes.
2 Drain the pineapple.
3 Dip each ring of pineapple into the batter and then with skewer, lower the ring into hot deep fat.
4 Cook until crisp and golden brown. Drain well and dredge with castor sugar mixed with a little cinnamon or ground ginger if liked.

Baked apples

cooking time 45 minutes - 1 hour

you will need:

4 large cooking apples	*Filling:*
2 oz. demerara sugar	2 oz. moist sugar creamed with 2 oz. butter
water	

1 Wash the apples and remove the core.
2 Slit round the skin of the apple with the tip of a knife about two-thirds up from the base.
3 Stand the apples in an ovenproof dish and fill centre with the creamed butter and sugar.
4 Sprinkle the apples with demerara sugar and add about ½ teacup water to the dish.
5 Bake in a moderate oven (350° F.—Mark 4) until the apples are soft.
6 Serve with cream.

Baked apple fillings

Apricot jam mixed with a few chopped, blanched almonds.

Mincemeat.

3 oz. chopped stoned dates mixed with honey and ½ teaspoon cinnamon.

3 oz. sultanas, currants or raisins mixed with 2 oz. sugar.

Apple snow

cooking time about 1½ hours
you will need:

2 lb. cooking apples	2 eggs
lemon rind	½ pint milk
4 oz. sugar	½ oz. castor sugar
1 tablespoon cream (optional)	2 oz. castor sugar

1 Peel, core and slice the apples. Stew with about ½ teacup water and the lemon rind until tender. Pass through a sieve.
2 Add the 4 oz. sugar and the cream if used.
3 Separate the eggs.
4 Heat the milk and pour on to the beaten yolks. Stir well, return to the pan and heat gently until the mixture thickens. Add the ½ oz. sugar.
5 Place the apple mixture in a buttered pie dish and pour the custard on top. Cook in a warm oven until set—about 40 minutes.
6 Whisk the egg whites until stiff and lightly fold in the remaining sugar.
7 Pile the meringue on top of the custard and return to a cool oven until the meringue is lightly coloured.

Swiss cream

cooking time 25 minutes
you will need:

4 oz. sponge cake or ratafia biscuits	1 lemon
3 – 4 tablespoons sherry	2 oz. castor sugar
1¼ oz. cornflour	¼ – ½ pint double cream
1 pint milk	chopped nuts

1 Place the sponge cake or the ratafia biscuits in the bottom of a dish or individual dishes and sprinkle with the sherry.
2 Blend the cornflour with a little of the milk to make a smooth cream.
3 Thinly peel the lemon and place the rind with the remaining milk in a saucepan and heat slowly.
4 Strain the milk on to the blended cornflour, stir and return to the saucepan. Cook gently for about 3 or 4 minutes. Stir in the sugar and allow to cool.
5 Lightly whip the cream and stir it into the cooled cornflour mixture with the juice of the lemon. If liked add more sugar.
6 Pour the mixture over the cake or biscuits and leave until cold. Decorate with chopped nuts.

If preferred, glacé cherries and angelica can be used instead of chopped nuts.

Summer pudding

you will need:

approximately 12 individual sponge cakes	1½ – 2 lb. any soft fruit or mixture of soft fruit
2 – 4 oz. sugar	

1 Cut the sponge cakes into inch-wide fingers and use to line the sides of a 1½-pint pudding basin or soufflé dish.
2 Cut triangles for lining the bottom.
3 Cook the chosen fruit with as little water as possible until it has become a pulp. Sweeten to taste.
4 Pour the fruit into the lined basin or dish. Cover the top with slices of sponge cake.
5 Cover with a saucer topped with a weight and leave until cold.
6 When cold turn out and coat with custard or fruit juice thickened to a coating consistency with arrowroot (1 level teaspoon to ½ pint juice).
7 Decorate the pudding with fruit or sliced almonds.

Cold lemon soufflé

you will need:

2 lemons	¼ pint water
3 – 4 eggs	½ pint double cream
5 oz. castor sugar	chopped pistachio nuts
½ oz. gelatine	

1 Prepare a china soufflé dish by tying a double band of greaseproof paper round it with 3 inches of the paper extending above the rim of the dish.
2 Whisk the egg yolks, sugar, lemon rind and juice in a bowl over hot water until the mixture is thick and creamy.
3 Remove the bowl from the hot water and whisk until cool.
4 Dissolve the gelatine in the water and half whip the cream.
5 Whisk the egg whites until stiff enough to stand in peaks.
6 Add the hot gelatine in a thin stream to the cooled egg mixture and stir until well blended.
7 Lightly fold in the cream and egg whites.
8 Using a metal spoon fold the mixture over very lightly and gently until just about to set.
9 Pour into the soufflé dish and leave to set.
10 When the soufflé is set, remove the paper band very carefully using the tip of a knife dipped in hot water if necessary to ease the paper away.
11 Decorate the sides of the soufflé with chopped pistachio nuts and if liked pipe the top with a little whipped cream.

Coffee cream

you will need:

3 egg yolks or 1 whole egg and 1 yolk	½ oz. gelatine
2 – 3 oz. castor sugar	4 tablespoons water
½ pint milk	2 – 3 teaspoons coffee essence
½ pint double cream	

1 Beat the eggs and sugar together in a bowl until sugar dissolves.
2 Heat the milk and pour on to the beaten eggs.
3 Strain back into the saucepan and cook until thick, stirring all the time. Allow to cool.
4 Dissolve the gelatine in the water and add with the coffee essence to the cooled custard. Stir well.
5 Whip the cream and fold lightly into the custard mixture just before it sets.
6 Pour into individual glasses or into a mould Leave in a cool place until set.

Cold chocolate soufflé

you will need:

1 oz. almonds	½ oz. gelatine
3 eggs	vanilla essence
2 oz. castor sugar	½ pint cream
2 oz. plain chocolate	chopped almonds
2 tablespoons water	whipped cream

1 Tie a double band of greaseproof paper round a soufflé dish so that the paper extends 2 - 3 inches above the rim.
2 Blanch the almonds, shred and brown them lightly in the oven.
3 Whisk the egg yolks and sugar over a pan of very hot water until thick and creamy. Remove from the heat.
4 Melt the chocolate in the water over a gentle heat, add the gelatine and continue heating until it is dissolved, then fold into the egg and sugar mixture.
5 Add the almonds, chopped, vanilla essence and lightly fold in the cream.
6 Beat the egg whites until stiff and fold into the mixture.
7 Pour into the prepared soufflé dish and leave to set.
8 Remove the paper band carefully and decorate with chopped almonds and whipped cream.

Strawberry shortcake

cooking time 30 - 40 minutes

you will need:

8 oz. self–raising flour	1 egg yolk
good pinch salt	strawberries
½ oz. ground almonds	½ pint double cream
4½ oz. margarine	sugar
2 oz. sugar	

1 Sieve the flour and salt into a bowl, add the ground almonds and mix well.
2 Cream the fat and sugar and beat in the egg yolk.
3 Work in the flour by hand, knead well.
4 Divide the mixture into three. Roll into rounds, a good ¼ inch thick.
5 Place each on a greased baking tray and bake in a moderate oven (350° F.—Mark 4) until golden (approximately 30 - 40 minutes).
6 Place on a wire tray until cold.
7 Sprinkle the strawberries with sugar to taste. Crush slightly with a fork, saving a few for decoration.
8 Whisk the cream until thick.
9 Mix three-quarters of the cream with the crushed strawberries.
10 Sandwich the layers of shortcake with the strawberry and cream mixture and decorate the top with the rest of the cream and the whole strawberries.

Apple shortcake

Prepare shortcake as above. Peel, core and slice 1 lb. cooking apples. Stew the apples with 4 oz. sugar, ¼ teaspoon cinnamon, grated rind of 1 lemon and 2 oz. sultanas. When cool, sandwich the shortcake with this filling. Decorate the top with whipped cream or dust with sugar. This filling may also be used to make an apple meringue pie. Fill a cooked flan case with the apple. Top with meringue and bake in a slow oven until the meringue is crisp.

Strawberry mousse

you will need:

4 oz. strawberries	½ pint double cream
1 oz. castor sugar	1 strawberry jelly

1 Sprinkle the strawberries with the sugar.
2 Dissolve the jelly in a little hot water and make up to ¾ pint with cold water.
3 When the jelly is almost set, whisk in the cream and continue whisking until the mixture is light and fluffy.
4 Mash the strawberries with a fork and fold lightly into jelly and cream mixture.
5 Pile the mixture into a bowl and leave in a cool place until set.
6 Decorate the mousse with more strawberries and serve very cold.

Chocolate mousse

you will need for each person:

2 oz. plain chocolate	1 teaspoon brandy (optional)
1 egg	1 tablespoon double cream (optional)

1 Break the chocolate into a bowl over a pan of hot water.
2 Separate the yolk of the egg from the white. Add the yolks and the brandy if used, to the chocolate.
3 Stir well and allow to heat gently until the mixture is fairly thick.
4 Remove from the heat and allow to cool. Do not allow to set.
7 Whip the cream, if used, and use to decorate cooled chocolate.
6 Pour into glasses.
7 Whip the cream, if used, and use to decorate the mousse.

Caramel custard

cooking time 1 - 1¼ hours

you will need:

4 oz. granulated sugar	1 oz. castor sugar
¼ pint water	½ pint evaporated milk
3 eggs	¼ pint water

1 Put the granulated sugar into a saucepan with the water and heat gently until the sugar is dissolved. Bring to the boil quickly and boil until the mixture becomes dark brown.
2 Pour into a 1½ pint mould or cake tin and tilt so that the bottom and sides are coated with the caramel.
3 Beat the eggs and castor sugar together lightly in a bowl.
4 Heat the milk and water together until blood heat. Pour on to the eggs and sugar, stir well and pour into the mould.
5 Cover with a piece of greased paper or foil and place in a tin containing about 1 inch water.
6 Bake in the centre of a slow oven (310° F.—Mark 2) until the custard is set.
7 Turn out on to a cold plate and serve at once.

Queen of puddings

cooking time 1¼ hours

you will need:

1 pint milk	2 oz. granulated sugar
4 oz. breadcrumbs	2 eggs
2 oz. butter or margarine	jam
grated rind 2 lemons	2 – 4 oz. castor sugar

1 Heat the milk and add the breadcrumbs, butter or margarine, lemon rind and granulated sugar. Leave to stand for 30 minutes.
2 Separate the whites from the yolks of the eggs and stir the yolks into the breadcrumb mixture.

3 Pour the mixture into a buttered pie dish and bake in a moderate oven (350° F.—Mark 4) for about 45 minutes until set.
4 When set, remove from the oven and spread with about 3 tablespoons jam.
5 Whisk the whites until stiff, add 1 oz. of the castor sugar and whisk again until stiff. Lightly stir in the rest of the sugar and pile the meringue over the jam.
6 Return to a very cool oven (265° F.—Mark ½) until the meringue is set and golden.

Savoy pudding

cooking time 1¼ hours

you will need:

8 oz. stale Savoy or sponge cake	1 wineglass sherry (optional)
2 oz. finely chopped mixed peel	4½ oz. castor sugar
½ pint milk	3 eggs
2 oz. melted butter	

1 Put the cake through a sieve. Add the mixed peel, milk, butter, sherry if used, and 1½ oz. of the sugar.
2 Separate the whites from the yolks of the eggs and add the yolks to the cake mixture. Beat thoroughly and pour the mixture into a buttered pie dish.
3 Bake in a moderate oven (350° F.—Mark 4) for about 45 minutes until set.
4 Whisk the whites until stiff.
5 Lightly fold in the remaining sugar and pile the meringue over the pudding.
6 Bake in a very cool oven until the meringue is set and golden brown—about 30 minutes.

Raspberry crunch pie

you will need:

3 oz. luxury margarine	*Filling:*
3 level dessertspoons golden syrup	¼ pint doube cream
6 oz. digestive biscuits, crushed	1 small punnet fresh raspberries with sugar to sweeten, or 1 packet frozen raspberries
1 oz. castor sugar	

1 Dissolve the margarine and syrup in a small saucepan and bring almost to the boil.
2 Put the crushed biscuits and sugar in a mixing bowl and add the melted mixture. Mix thoroughly together. Allow to cool slightly.
3 Knead well and press into a 7-inch pie plate. Leave in a cool place until firm.
4 Whisk the cream until stiff.
5 Fold in the raspberries, reserving a few for decoration.
6 Add the sugar if used.
7 Pile the mixture into prepared case and decorate with raspberries.
8 Serve at once.

Fruit Alaska

you will need:

1 cooked flan case	2 egg whites
1 small can pineapple cubes	2 oz. granulated sugar
few strawberries	2 oz. castor sugar
1 block ice cream	

1 Place the flan case on an ovenproof plate.
2 Drain the pineapple well and place in the flan case with strawberries.
3 Whisk the egg whites until stiff. Add the granulated sugar and continue whisking until the mixture is stiff and dry.
4 Lightly fold in the castor sugar.
5 Place the block of ice cream on the fruit and cover with meringue, making sure that it comes right down to the edge of the flan case.
6 Bake in a very hot oven (450° F.—Mark 8) for 3 - 4 minutes until the meringue is lightly streaked with gold. Serve at once.

Pancakes

you will need:

8 oz. plain flour	cooking fat
¼ teaspoon salt	lemon
2 eggs	castor sugar
1 pint milk	

1 Sieve the flour and salt into a mixing bowl. Make a well in the centre and break the eggs into this.
2 Add about ¼ pint of the milk and stir, gradually working in the flour from the sides.
3 Add enough milk to give a stiff batter consistency. Beat thoroughly for at least 5 minutes, then cover, and leave to stand for 30 minutes.
4 Add the remaining milk and stir well. Pour the mixture into a jug.
5 Melt about ¼ oz. fat in a small clean frying pan or omelette pan.
6 Just as the fat is beginning to smoke, pour in just enough batter to cover the bottom of the pan thinly. Tilt the pan to ensure the batter runs over evenly.
7 Move the frying pan gently over a quick heat until the pancake is set and brown underneath. Make sure it is loose at the sides and turn it over with a fish slice or a broad-bladed knife.
8 Brown on the other side and turn on to a sugared sheet of greaseproof paper. Sprinkle with sugar and lemon juice and roll up. Keep hot while cooking the rest.
9 Serve the pancakes sprinkled with castor sugar and accompanied by wedges of lemon.
This makes about 12 pancakes.

Jam pancakes

Make the pancakes as for plain pancakes and spread with jam before rolling up.

Brandy pancakes

Make the pancakes as for plain pancakes and spread with the following filling before rolling up.
Cream 2 oz. butter with 1 oz. castor sugar until white. Beat in 1 tablespoon brandy and 1 teaspoon lemon juice.

Crêpes Suzette

you will need:

½ pint batter (as for pancakes)	grated rind ½ orange
icing sugar	2 teaspoons orange juice
brandy or rum	1 teaspoon lemon juice
2 oz. butter	1 tablespoon kirsch or curaçao
3 oz. castor sugar	

1 Make batter and leave to stand for 30 minutes
2 Cream the butter and castor sugar together until white and soft. Beat in the orange rind and juice, lemon juice and the liqueur.
3 Make very thin pancakes, spreading each with a little of the filling before rolling up. Dredge each with a little icing sugar and keep warm.
4 When all the pancakes are made, pour on some brandy or rum and set alight. Serve at once.

Hot soufflés
Preparing the tin or mould

Grease the tin or mould with a little clarified butter. Tie a double band of greased paper round the tin or mould so that it stands at least 3 inches above the rim. This is to hold the mixture as it rises. Have the cut edges of the paper at the top. When steaming a soufflé, cut a circle of greased paper for the top of the tin or mould to prevent any water dripping on the soufflé while it is cooking.

Soufflés can be steamed in a steamer or in a saucepan with enough boiling water to come half way up the side of the pan. Stand the soufflé tin on an upturned plate or saucer. Steam gently but steadily and avoid moving the steamer. When the soufflé is cooked, it should be well risen and just firm to the touch. Turn the soufflé out on to a hot dish and serve at once.

Baked soufflés are served in the dish in which they are cooked. They can be cooked in one large dish or in individual dishes. Grease as for steamed soufflés. It is not necessary to tie paper round the case as the soufflé becomes firm as it rises. Fill the dish only three-quarters full, and avoid opening the oven door whilst the soufflé is cooking. A sudden draught of cold air could cause the mixture to sink. The soufflé, when cooked, should be well risen and firm to the touch.

Chocolate soufflé

cooking time about 1 hour

you will need:

2 oz. plain chocolate	4 egg yolks
7½ fluid oz. milk	3 oz. castor sugar
1½ oz. butter	½ teaspoon vanilla essence
1½ oz. plain flour	5 egg whites

1 Prepare a soufflé tin ready for steaming.
2 Grate the chocolate finely and dissolve it in the milk.
3 Melt the butter, stir in the flour and cook for a few minutes. Do not allow to become brown.
4 Add the milk and beat well until smooth. Reheat until the mixture becomes thick and will leave the sides of the pan.
5 Cool slightly and beat in the egg yolks, one at a time. Add the sugar and essence.
6 Whisk the egg whites until they are stiff enough to stand up in points.
7 Fold carefully into the mixture, taking care not to push out the air.
8 Turn the mixture into the prepared mould and steam very gently until the soufflé is just firm to the touch and well risen. Or bake in hot oven for about 40 minutes.
9 Turn out and serve at once.

Raspberry soufflé

cooking time 25 - 30 minutes

you will need:

8 oz. ripe raspberries	½ teacup cream
2 oz. cornflour	3 eggs
2 oz. castor sugar	2 oz. cake crumbs

1 Butter a soufflé dish.
2 Sieve the raspberries and mix with the cornflour and sugar, stirring until smooth.
3 Add the cream, the egg yolks and cake crumbs.
4 Whisk the egg whites until stiff and fold them into the mixture.
5 Turn the mixture into the prepared soufflé dish and bake in a moderately hot oven (375° F.—Mark 5) until well risen and firm.

Chantilly soufflé

cooking time about 35 minutes

you will need:

1 pint milk	finely grated rind
2 tablespoons sugar	orange
2 rounded tablespoons	3 large eggs
fine semolina	strawberries

1 Warm the milk, sprinkle in the sugar and the semolina.
2 Bring to the boil, stirring all the time.
3 Remove from the heat and stir in the orange rind. Allow to cool slightly, then beat in the egg yolks.
4 Whisk the egg whites until stiff and fold gently into milk mixture.
5 Turn the mixture into a greased 6-inch soufflé dish and bake in a hot oven (400° F.—Mark 6) for about 35 minutes.
6 Meanwhile, slice the strawberries and sprinkle them with castor sugar.
7 Remove the soufflé from the oven, spoon the sugared strawberries over the top and serve at once.

Sandwiches and Sandwich Fillings

Party sandwiches can be made hours before or even the day before they are to be used if they are well wrapped (in polythene bags, tinfoil or greaseproof paper) covered with a damp cloth and kept in the refrigerator or a cool place.
Butter for spreading should be well softened. Keep it in a warmish place or beat 1 dessertspoon hot water in each 4 oz. for a creamy spread that will not harden.

Seasoned butters for sandwiches

To each 4 oz. butter beat in:
1 tablespoon chutney, 1 oz. grated cheddar cheese.
1 tablespoon anchovy essence, the rind and juice 1 lemon.
1 tablespoon chopped almonds, 1 teaspoon powdered ginger.
1 dessertspoon curry powder, 1 teaspoon dried marjoram.
1 tablespoon tomato purée, 1 teaspoon castor sugar, 1 dessertspoon dried basil and ½ teaspoon made mustard.

Sandwich spreads

Chopped hard-boiled egg with mayonnaise and curry powder.
Chopped anchovy fillets with cream or cottage cheese.
Flaked salmon with capers, salad cream and minced onion.

Lightly boiled frankfurter chunks in mustard-flavoured mayonnaise.

Shrimps, chopped fried bacon, thick cream and onion salt.

Peanut butter and redcurrant jelly spiced with ginger.

Chopped nuts, celery and sliced banana mixed with apple sauce.

Sandwich and bridge roll fillings

Egg fillings:

Chop hard-boiled eggs, mix with chopped diced crisp bacon and a little salad dressing or mayonnaise.

Chop hard-boiled eggs, mix with sweet chutney and chopped watercress.

Scramble eggs, mix with chopped chives and a little sliced tomato.

Chop soft-boiled eggs finely—mix with butter and seasoning.

Cheese fillings:

Cream cheese, mix with a little well-drained and finely-chopped pineapple.

Cream cheese, mix with chopped walnuts, spread on crisp lettuce.

Slice of Gruyére or Cheddar cheese spread lightly with made mustard and sprigs of watercress.

Grate cheese, mix with grated raw carrot and little mayonnaise.

Fish fillings:

Mix chopped cooked cod's roe with a little mayonnaise, celery, salt and chopped watercress.

Mash sardines and mix with finely diced or sliced cucumber and a little lemon juice.

Mash tuna fish well, mix with chopped skinned tomatoes, chopped watercress, moisten with a little mayonnaise, season well.

Spread canned well-drained salmon on crisp lettuce, then spread lightly with horseradish cream, sprinkled with grated cheese.

Cook kippers lightly, flake flesh from bones, season well, add a little lemon juice or vinegar and mix with butter and chopped watercress.

Meat fillings

Flake corned beef, mix with sweet chutney or mustard, mayonnaise and chopped spring onion.

Flake corned beef, mix with sweet chutney or chopped pickle and a little grated cheese.

Chop tongue finely, mix with a little mayonnaise, good pinch of curry powder and chopped hard-boiled egg.

Chop cooked ham or boiled bacon, mix with skinned chopped tomatoes and shredded lettuce. If necessary add a little mayonnaise.

Chop luncheon meat and mix with chopped watercress. Bind with soft cream cheese.

Cover crisp lettuce with thin slices of luncheon meat. Spread lightly with redcurrant jelly or stoned chopped prunes.

Other fillings

Anchovy and egg: Blend 1 can anchovies, finely-chopped, 4 chopped hard-boiled eggs, 1 tablespoon mayonnaise and 4 oz. soft margarine.

Bacon and chutney: Blend 8 oz. streaky bacon, chopped and cooked, 2 tablespoons chutney, 4 oz. soft margarine.

Ham and tomato: Blend 8 oz. minced ham, 8 oz. skinned chopped tomatoes, 4 oz. soft margarine, seasoning.

Cheese and pineapple: Blend two 4 oz. packets cream or cottage cheese, 1 small can pineapple pieces, drained and chopped, 2 oz. soft margarine.

Liver sausage and onion: Blend 8 oz. liver sausage, 3 - 4 spring onions finely chopped, 4 oz. soft margarine, seasoning.

Cheese and celery: Blend 4 oz. finely grated cheese, 2 finely chopped sticks of celery or 1 head of chicory, finely chopped, 4 oz. soft margarine, seasoning.

Quantity guide

Sliced white sandwich loaf gives approximately 24 slices.

Sliced brown loaf gives approximately 18 slices.

4 oz. butter or margarine will cover approximately 24 slices of bread (soften before using).

8 oz. butter will cover approximately 50 small bridge rolls (100 halves).

2 lb. grated cheese will fill 36 sandwiches.

24 hard-boiled eggs mixed with mayonnaise will fill 36 sandwiches.

2 lb. sliced meat will fill 3 dozen full sandwich rounds.

For a sandwich meal allow $1\frac{1}{2}$ - 2 full rounds or 8 - 10 small sandwiches per person.

Scones and Pastries

Scones

cooking time small scones 7 - 10 minutes
             scone round 10 - 15 minutes

you will need:

8 oz. flour	1 oz. sugar
2 teaspoons baking powder	½ teaspoon salt
¼ pint milk	beaten egg or milk for
2 oz. fat (butter,	glazing
margarine or lard)	

1 Grease and flour a baking tray.
2 Sieve flour, baking powder and salt.
3 Rub the fat into the flour with the finger-tips.
4 Add the sugar and any other ingredients to be used (see following recipes).
5 Stir in the milk and mix quickly to a soft dough.
6 Turn out on to a floured surface. Flour hands and form into a ball. Cut into two pieces.
7 Press each lightly by hand, or roll, into a round ¾ inch thick.
8 Cut out with a 2-inch cutter or divide each round into quarters with a sharp knife. Do not cut through.
9 Place on the baking tray, brush with beaten egg or milk.
10 Bake in a hot oven (425° F.—Mark 7).
11 Cool on a wire tray. Serve hot or cold.

Cheese scones

Make as for basic recipe, omitting the sugar and adding 4 oz. grated cheese and a pinch of dry mustard.

Fancy scones

Make as for basic recipe, adding 1 oz. chopped mixed peel and 1 oz. chopped glacé cherries.

Fruit scones

Make as for basic recipe, adding 2 oz. currants, sultanas or raisins.

Tea scones

Add 1 beaten egg to the basic recipe and use a little less milk. Serve hot with butter or cream and strawberry or raspberry jam.

Girdle scones

Use basic recipe. Divide each large piece of dough into 8 sections. Heat a girdle, the hot plate of an electric cooker, the oven sheet of a cooker or a frying pan, until moderately hot. Grease well. Cook scones for 4 - 5 minutes on each side. Serve hot.

Drop scones or Scotch pancakes

cooking time 6 minutes

Use basic scone recipe adding 1 egg and increasing milk to ½ pint.

1 Beat the liquid into the dry ingredients to make a thick batter.
2 Drop the mixture in small spoonfuls on to a moderately hot girdle, which has been well greased.
3 When bubbles rise to the surface and the underside is lightly browned, turn scones over with a palette knife. Cook gently until cooked through.
4 Place at once in a clean tea towel to keep moist. Serve hot with butter, honey or treacle.

Shortcrust pastry

you will need:

8 oz. flour	2 oz. lard (or vege-
pinch salt	table shortening)
2 oz. margarine	cold water to mix

1 Sieve the flour and salt into a mixing bowl.
2 Chop the fat roughly and add to the flour. Rub the fat into the flour using the finger-tips, until the mixture resembles breadcrumbs.
3 Add cold water gradually and knead mixture lightly by hand until it works together into a firm dough.
4 Turn out on to a lightly floured surface and knead lightly until smooth. Turn pastry over and roll out as required.

Rich shortcrust pastry or flan pastry

you will need:

8 oz. flour	1 teaspoon castor sugar
pinch salt	1 egg yolk
5 oz. butter	1 - 2 tablespoons cold water

1 Sieve flour and salt into a bowl.
2 Rub the butter lightly into the flour, using the finger-tips until mixture resembles breadcrumbs.
3 Add sugar and egg yolk, work into the flour, adding water gradually, until mixture forms a firm dough.
4 Turn on to a floured surface, knead lightly and roll out.

If the pastry is difficult to handle, leave in a cold place for at least 30 minutes before using.

To make a flan case

1 Make pastry as above.
2 Roll out pastry into a circle about 2 inches larger than the flan ring.
3 Place flan ring on a baking sheet. Place the round of pastry over the ring and press into shape, taking care that the pastry fits well against the inside edge, but that it is not stretched.
4 Trim off surplus pastry by passing the rolling pin over the edge of the ring. Place a piece of lightly-greased paper, greased side down, in the flan case and fill the flan with uncooked rice, haricot beans or macaroni.
5 Bake in a hot oven (400° F—Mark 6) until the pastry is firm—15 minutes. Pastry baked in this way is described as 'baked blind'. This is done to ensure a good shape. The rice, etc., can be stored in a jar and used indefinitely for this purpose.
6 Remove the filling and paper from flan. Return flan to the oven for a further 5 minutes to allow base to cook through.
7 Remove flan ring and leave flan case on a wire tray until cold.
Cold cooked pastry cases can be stored in an airtight tin and used as required.
If a flan ring is not available, a sandwich tin may be used, but strips of paper should be placed across the inside of the tin to protrude at the edge, before the pastry is fitted. This will enable the flan case to be easily removed from the tin after cooking.

Flaky pastry

you will need:

8 oz. flour	squeeze lemon juice
pinch salt	cold water to mix
6 oz. fat (butter or equal quantities of margarine and lard)	

1 Sieve flour and salt into a bowl.
2 Cream the fat until soft and pliable and divide into 4 portions.
3 Rub one portion of the fat into the flour, add a squeeze of lemon juice and sufficient cold water to make a soft dough.
4 Roll the dough into an oblong. Cover two-thirds of the oblong with another portion of fat, dabbing the fat in small pieces over the dough.
5 Fold the dough in three, starting at the bottom with the uncovered section. Bring this up to the centre of the oblong. Bring the top third down over this. Lightly press the edges together with the rolling pin.
6 Half turn the pastry to the left and roll it out into an oblong.

7 Repeat this process (5 and 6) twice, adding another portion of fat each time.
8 Fold the pastry in three once more without adding fat.
9 Wrap it in greaseproof paper or foil, and leave in the 'fridge' or a cold place for an hour before rolling out for use.
10 If possible, leave the pastry to 'relax' in a cool place for about 10 minutes between each rolling.

Rough puff pastry

you will need:

8 oz. flour	1 teaspoon lemon juice
pinch salt	cold water to mix
6 oz. butter or equal quantities of margarine and lard	

1 Sieve the flour and salt into a bowl.
2 Cut the fat into small cubes, add to the flour. Do not rub in.
3 Add lemon juice and sufficient cold water to mix to a fairly stiff dough.
4 Roll out into an oblong, taking care not to stretch the pastry at the edges.
5 Fold the pastry into three. Bring the bottom end two-thirds up and the top piece down to the folded edge.
6 Seal the edges by pressing lightly with a rolling pin.
7 Half turn the pastry to the left and roll it out into an oblong.
8 Repeat this process (5 and 6) twice.
9 Fold the pastry in three once more. Wrap it in greaseproof paper or foil and leave in a 'fridge' or cold place for an hour before rolling out for use.
This pastry is very similar to puff pastry but is easier and quicker to make. It can be used in any recipe that requires puff or flaky pastry.

Petites mille feuilles

cooking time 8 minutes
you will need:

6 oz. rough puff pastry	$\frac{1}{4}$ pint double cream
1 egg	almonds, blanched and
apricot jam	chopped

1 Roll out pastry $\frac{1}{8}$ inch thick.
2 Cut into small rounds using a 2-inch cutter. Place on a baking tray.
3 Brush with beaten egg and prick with a fork.
4 Bake in a very hot oven (470° F.—Mark 9) until golden brown.
5 Cool on a wire tray. Sandwich 3 rounds of pastry with apricot jam and cream, whisked until thick.
6 Brush top of each lightly with jam and sprinkle with nuts.

Petites lemon mille feuilles

Make as above. Sandwich layers of pastry with lemon curd and cream. Spoon a little lemon flavoured glacé icing on the top of each and sprinkle with nuts.

Raspberry mille feuilles

Cut 4 rounds of rough pastry about 8 inches in diameter. Bake in a very hot oven for about 10 minutes. When cold, sandwich with crushed raspberries, sprinkled with castor sugar and whipped cream. Cover top with glacé icing and decorate with whole raspberries or almonds.

Cream horns

Roll flaky or rough puff pastry thinly into an oblong 12 inches long. Cut into 1-inch strips. Moisten edges of each strip and roll round a cream horn tin. Start at the pointed end of the tin and overlap the pastry slightly. Bake in a very hot oven (470° F.—Mark 9) until crisp (10 - 15 minutes). Slip off tins and leave until cold. Place a good spoonful of jam in each and fill up with whipped cream. Dredge with icing sugar.

Almond pastries

Line boat shaped or patty tins with rough puff pastry. Half fill with soft almond paste. Cover with a pastry top, seal and flute the edges. Brush with beaten egg. Make 2 or 3 small cuts in the top of each and bake at 425° F.—Mark 7 for 20 - 30 minutes. Dredge with icing sugar and serve hot or cold.

Danish almond pastries

Make as above, placing a little chopped mixed peel in each pastry case before adding the almond paste. When pastries are cold, coat top of each with lemon flavoured glacé icing.

Nut and spice twists – a good way to use up scraps of pastry

Roll out rough puff or flaky pastry thinly. Cut into strips 1½ inches wide and 3 inches long. Brush with egg white and sprinkle with chopped almonds and a pinch of mixed spice or cinnamon. Twist each strip at either end. Bake in a very hot oven until golden brown (5 - 8 minutes). Dredge with icing sugar.

Jam puffs

Roll out rough puff pastry thinly (⅛ inch thick) and cut into 4 rounds. Spread jam over half of each. Brush edges of circle with beaten egg, fold over and seal. 'Knock up' with the back

of a knife and make small flutes around the edge. Brush with beaten egg, sprinkle with castor sugar, make one or two slits in the top of each and bake in a very hot oven for about 10 minutes, until golden brown.

Apple puffs

Make as for jam puffs, using sweetened apple purée instead of jam. Sprinkle the puffs with castor sugar mixed with a little cinnamon.

Cream slices

cooking time 10 - 15 minutes
you will need:

6 oz. rough puff pastry	whipped cream or
raspberry or strawberry	confectioners custard
jam	white glacé icing

1 Roll out the pastry ¼ inch thick, into a strip 4 inches wide.
2 Cut into 1½ inch pieces and place on a baking sheet. Bake in a very hot oven (470° F.—Mark 9) until well risen and golden. Leave to cool on a wire tray.
3 When cold, sandwich 2 slices together with jam and cream or custard.
4 Coat the top of each with glacé icing.

French cream slices

Make as above. Sprinkle the glacé icing with slivers of toasted almonds. When icing sets, dredge each slice with dry icing sugar.

Lemon hearts

Roll pastry out into a piece one-quarter inch thick. Cut out with a heart-shaped cutter. Bake in a very hot oven for 10 minutes. When cold, cut through with a sharp knife and sandwich together with lemon curd. Coat top with lemon glacé icing and decorate with small pieces of angelica and halved glacé cherries.

Devonshire hearts

Make as for lemon hearts. Sandwich pastry with strawberry jam and whipped cream. Dredge with icing sugar before serving.

Maids of honour

cooking time 25 - 30 minutes
you will need:

4 oz. puff pastry	½ oz. flour
4 oz. ground almonds	2 tablespoons cream
2 oz. castor sugar	1 tablespoon orange
1 egg	flower water—this is
	available from chemists

1 Roll out the pastry thinly and line 12 patty tins.
2 Mix the ground almonds and castor sugar together.

3 Beat in the egg, flour, cream and orange flower water.

4 Put a little of the mixture into each patty case.

5 Bake in a hot oven (400° F.—Mark 6) until set and golden brown.

6 Cool on a wire tray.

Frangipane tart

cooking time 25 - 30 minutes

you will need:

4 oz. rich shortcrust pastry	1 teaspoon flour
2 oz. sugar	2 oz. ground almonds
2 oz. butter	icing sugar or glacé
1 egg	icing

1 Line a 7-inch pie plate with pastry.

2 Cream the fat and sugar and beat in the egg.

3 Stir in the flour and ground almonds.

4 Spread the almond mixture into the pastry case.

5 Bake in a moderate oven (350° F.—Mark 4).

6 Leave until cold, then dust with icing sugar or spread with lemon flavoured glacé icing.

Canadian apple tart

cooking time 30 - 40 minutes

you will need:

6 oz. shortcrust pastry	4 oz. brown sugar
1 lb. cooking apples	1 oz. butter

1 Line an 8-inch pie plate with pastry and prick well with a fork.

2 Peel and core the apples, cut into slices and arrange over the pastry.

3 Sprinkle thickly with sugar and dot with butter.

4 Bake in a hot oven (425° F.—Mark 7) for 10 minutes, then reduce heat to 400° F.—Mark 6 and cook until golden. Serve hot or cold.

Florentine tart

Prepare as above, baking the pastry case 'blind'. Stew the apples with sugar and grated nutmeg to taste. Allow the apples to cool. Spread over the pastry and top with meringue (made from 2 egg whites and 4 oz. sugar). Bake in a cool oven until meringue is firm.

Mince pies

1 Roll out flaky, rough puff or shortcrust pastry about ⅛ inch thick.

2 Cut out enough small rounds of pastry to make a lid for each pie.

3 Knead all the scraps of pastry lightly together and roll out.

4 Cut out rounds to line patty tins, making them a size larger than the tin.

5 Line the tins with pastry, fill with mincemeat and damp the edges.

6 Put on the lids, seal and flute the edges. Make a small hole in the centre of each.

7 Brush each pie with egg white and sprinkle with sugar.

8 Bake in a very hot oven (450° F.—Mark 8) for 20 - 30 minutes if using flaky or rough puff pastry. Bake at 400° F.—Mark 6 if using shortcrust pastry.

Cheese pastry

you will need:

4 oz. flour	2 oz. grated cheese
salt and cayenne pepper	1 egg yolk
2 oz. butter	

1 Sieve dry ingredients and rub in fat very lightly with the finger-tips. Add cheese and mix well.

2 Beat the egg yolk with about 1 tablespoon water and mix into the dry ingredients to give a stiff dough. Knead lightly and use as required for biscuits, etc.

Cheese straws

1 Roll out some cheese pastry thinly and cut in fingers measuring about 3 inches long and ¼ inch wide. Stamp out a few pastry rings, using 2 cutters, and bake in a hot oven (400° F.—Mark 6) for about 10 minutes.

2 When cold, the straws may be threaded through the rings.

Choux pastry (basic recipe)

you will need:

¼ pint water	2 oz. flour
1 oz. butter	1 egg
pinch salt	1 egg yolk

1 Heat the water and butter with the salt in a small pan.

2 Bring to the boil, add the flour and beat well with a wooden spoon.

3 Remove from the heat and continue beating until mixture is smooth and leaves the sides of the pan.

4 Allow to cool, then beat in the egg mixture gradually.

Chocolate éclairs

cooking time 30 - 35 minutes

1 Make choux pastry as above.

2 Put mixture into a piping bag with a ½-inch plain nozzle.

3 Pipe in six 3-inch lengths on a greased baking tray.

4 Bake in a fairly hot oven (400° F.—Mark 6).

5 Remove from tray, make a small slit in the side of each to allow the steam to escape.

6 When cool, fill each with sweetened whipped cream.

7 Coat the top of each éclair with chocolate glacé icing (see page 80).

Savoury éclairs

Make as for chocolate éclairs, when cold fill with savoury filling (see page 28). If liked, the top of each may be glazed with a little melted aspic jelly and sprinkled with chopped parsley or paprika.

Cream buns

cooking time 20 - 30 minutes

1 Make basic choux pastry (see page 71).
2 Put into a piping bag with a half-inch plain nozzle.
3 Pipe in 6 small rounds at least 3 inches apart on a greased baking sheet. Cover with an inverted roasting tin.
4 Bake in a hot oven (400° F.—Mark 6).
5 Remove on to a wire tray making a small slit in the side of each to allow the steam to escape.
6 When cool, fill each with sweetened whipped cream or confectioner's custard (see page 13).
7 Dredge each with icing sugar or coat top with coffee glacé icing.

Profiteroles

cooking time 30 - 35 minutes

1 Make basic choux pastry (see page 71).
2 Pipe with a ¼-inch plain nozzle in 4 rounds on a greased baking tray. Cover with an inverted roasting tin.
3 Bake in a hot oven (400° F.—Mark 6).
4 Remove on to a wire tray to cool, making a slit in each to allow the steam to escape.
5 Fill each with whipped cream.
6 Serve coated with hot chocolate sauce.

Sandwich and Sponge Cakes

Neapolitan layer cake

cooking time 35 - 45 minutes

you will need:

8 oz. soft margarine	6 oz. luxury margarine
8 oz. castor sugar	2 tablespoons milk
4 eggs	2 oz. glacé cherries
8 oz. self-raising flour	1 oz. walnuts
Filling:	2 pineapple rings, well
1 lb. icing sugar, sieved	drained
	1 stick angelica

1 Place all the cake ingredients together in a mixing bowl.
2 Beat for 1 minute with a wooden spoon.
3 Place the mixture in two 8-inch sandwich tins, greased and the bottom lined with greaseproof paper. Smooth the top of the mixture.
4 Bake in the middle of a very moderate oven (335° F.—Mark 3). Cool on a wire tray.
5 Place the icing sugar, margarine and milk in a mixing bowl. Beat thoroughly together.
6 Chop the cherries (reserving 2 for decoration) walnuts, pineapple and angelica. Mix together and add to the filling. Beat thoroughly.
7 Cut through the centre of each cake.
8 Sandwich together with the filling (keeping enough for the top) making three layers of filling.
9 Spread the remaining filling on top of the cake.
10 Decorate with the remaining chopped cherries.

Swiss roll

cooking time 7 - 9 minutes

you will need:

3 eggs	1 tablespoon hot water
4 oz. castor sugar	warmed jam
4 oz. flour	

1 Grease a Swiss roll tin (9 × 13 inches) and line with greased greaseproof paper, cut 2 inches larger all round than the tin.
2 Sieve the flour.
3 Whisk the eggs and sugar in a large bowl over a pan of hot water. Continue whisking until the mixture is thick and fluffy and stiff enough to hold the impression of the whisk for a few seconds. Remove from over the hot water.
4 Stir in the water and lightly fold in the flour.
5 Put the mixture into the prepared tin, tilting the tin so that the mixture is spread evenly.
6 Bake in a hot oven (425° F.—Mark 7) until golden and springy to touch.
7 Spread a sheet of greaseproof or a damp clean tea towel with castor sugar. Turn the roll out on to this and remove the paper.
8 Using a sharp knife, trim all the crisp outer edges, keeping the shape as neat as possible.
9 Quickly spread the surface of the roll with warmed jam to within ½ inch of the edge.

10 Make a long cut half way through the depth of the sponge, 1 inch from the near end of the sponge. Roll up the sponge as tightly as possible, using the paper or cloth to help keep the roll.

11 Cool on a wire tray and sprinkle with castor sugar.

Sponge flan

cooking time 10 minutes

you will need:

3 eggs	3 oz. flour
3 oz. castor sugar	pinch salt

1 Brush an 8-inch sponge flan tin with melted fat or oil. Dust with flour.

2 Sieve the flour and salt.

3 Break eggs into a large bowl, add sugar.

4 Place bowl over a pan of hot water and whisk with a wire or rotary beater until the mixture is thick and becomes light in colour.

5 Remove from the heat and continue whisking until mixture holds the marks made by the whisk—about 1 minute.

6 Fold in half the flour, mixing it in lightly. Add remainder in the same way.

7 Pour into the prepared tin and bake in a hot oven (425° F.—Mark 7) until golden and springy to the touch.

8 Turn out on to a wire tray. Fill when cold.

Oriental flan

Bake flan case as above. Drain 1 can mandarin oranges. Arrange the oranges in circles in the flan case. Dissolve half a lemon jelly in a little hot water and make up to $\frac{1}{2}$ pint with juice from the oranges. Leave the jelly until almost setting and then spoon over the fruit and leave to set. Decorate flan with whipped cream and stud with slices of crystallised ginger if liked.

Fruit salad flan

Bake flan case as above. Fill with assorted fruit, fresh and canned. Fresh fruit should be prepared according to kind (e.g. cherries—stoned, grapes—seeded, etc.) and canned fruit should be well drained. Cover with glaze and leave to set in a cool place.

Glaze for fruit flans

Use 2 teaspoons arrowroot and $\frac{1}{4}$ pint sweetened fruit juice or syrup made from $\frac{1}{4}$ pint water and 2 oz. sugar. Blend arrowroot with a little of the liquid. Bring remaining liquid to the boil, stir into blended arrowroot. Return to the heat and boil for 1 - 2 minutes until clear.

Add a few drops of colouring or lemon juice if liked. Allow to cool, then spoon carefully over the fruit and leave to set.

Victoria sandwich

cooking time 25 minutes

you will need:

4 oz. butter or margarine	4 oz. self-raising flour
4 oz. sugar	water or milk—about
2 eggs	1 tablespoon
	(optional)*

1 Grease two 7-inch sandwich tins and dust with flour.

2 Cream the fat and sugar till white and creamy.

3 Beat in the eggs gradually.

4 Fold in the sieved flour.

5 Divide between the two tins, making sure the mixture is level.

6 Bake on the top shelf of a moderately hot oven (375° F.—Mark 5).

7 Turn out on to a wire tray to cool. When cold, sandwich together with jam and dust the top with sugar.

* If large eggs are used, additional liquid is not necessary, but water or milk may be added with the egg to give a soft dropping consistency.

For 8-inch sandwich tins you will need 3 eggs and 6 oz. fat, sugar and self-raising flour. Bake for 30 - 35 minutes.

Sponge cake

cooking time 10 - 12 minutes

you will need:

3 large eggs	4 oz. sugar
3 oz. flour ($\frac{1}{2}$ level teaspoon baking powder may be added to the flour)	1 tablespoon hot water
	1 oz. butter or margarine (optional)

1 Melt fat if used. It should be pourable but not hot.

2 Grease and flour two 7-inch sandwich tins.

3 Sieve flour and baking powder if used.

4 Put eggs and sugar in a bowl over hot water, and whisk until thick and creamy.

5 Remove from the heat and fold in the flour.

6 Stir in water and fat, if used.

7 Divide between tins, bake near the top of a very hot oven (425° F.—Mark 7).

8 Remove cakes from oven when firm, leave in the tins for 1 or 2 minutes, turn on to a wire tray to cool.

9 When cold, sandwich with jam or a creamy filling and dust the top with sugar.

Genoese sponge

cooking time about 45 minutes

you will need:

3 oz. butter	3 large eggs
2½ oz. self-raising flour	4 oz. sugar
¼ oz. cornflour	

1 Clarify the butter.
2 Grease and line an oblong tin, 10 × 7 × 1 inch deep.
3 Sieve flour and salt.
4 Put eggs and sugar into a large bowl and place the bowl over a pan of hot water. Whisk until the mixture is light and thick and will retain the impression of the whisk.
5 Remove bowl from the heat and very lightly fold in half the flour.
6 Fold in the remaining flour alternately with the cooled butter.
7 Bake in a moderately hot oven (375° F.— Mark 5) until golden brown and firm to the touch.
8 Turn on to a wire tray to cool.
This mixture may be used to make oblong layer cakes or gâteaux. Make as many layers as required and when cold, sandwich together with whipped cream or butter cream. Coat with glacé icing or frosting and decorate as liked. Alternatively, cut the sponge into fingers or fancy shapes when cold. Ice and decorate as liked.

Coffee cream cake

cooking time 30 - 35 minutes

you will need:

8 oz. butter	*Coffee cream:*
8 oz. sugar	6 oz. butter
rind and juice 1 small lemon	12 oz. icing sugar
4 eggs	4 heaped teaspoons instant coffee
8 oz. self-raising flour	1 dessertspoon boiling water
pinch salt	
1 tablespoon water	2 oz. walnuts, chopped

1 Grease and line two 8-inch sandwich tins and line the bottom of each with a round of grease-proof paper.
2 Sieve the flour and salt.
3 Cream the fat and sugar, add the lemon rind, finely grated.
4 Separate the egg yolks from the whites. Beat yolks into the creamed mixture a little at a time.
5 Fold in the flour, adding the lemon juice and water to make a soft dropping consistency.
6 Whisk egg whites until stiff, fold into the mixture.

7 Divide the mixture between the two tins, smooth the tops with a palette knife.
8 Bake in a moderately hot oven (375° F.— Mark 5) until golden.
9 Turn out on to a wire tray and leave until cold.
10 Make the coffee cream by creaming the butter until soft.
11 Add the sieved icing sugar and beat until smooth.
12 Dissolve the coffee in the boiling water and beat into the creamed butter and sugar.
13 Add the chopped walnuts and mix thoroughly.
14 Sandwich the cold cakes together with some of the coffee cream and place the rest on top of the cake, roughing it up slightly with a fork.

To clarify butter

Place butter in a pan with cold water. Heat slowly until the butter melts. Strain into a bowl and leave until the butter sets on top of the water. Remove the butter and scrape off the sediment from the underside. Put the clarified butter in a small bowl and leave in a warm place so that it is melted and ready for use. Do not allow to become hot.

For the unexpected guest

Quick mix cakes

These 'minute-mix' cakes are made in one stage. No creaming is required. Their success depends on the use of a quick creaming fat, so choose soft or superfine margarine.

Orange layer cake
you will need:

8 oz. self-raising flour	3 eggs
pinch salt	rind 1 orange, finely grated
1 level teaspoon baking powder	about 3 tablespoons milk
6 oz. castor sugar	
6 oz. margarine	

Lemon layer cake
you will need:

The same ingredients as for orange layer cake using lemon rind instead of orange rind.

Chocolate cake
you will need:

6 oz. self-raising flour	6 oz. margarine
pinch salt	3 eggs
4 level tablespoons cocoa	¼ teaspoon vanilla essence
small pinch bicarbonate of soda	about 3 tablespoons milk
6 oz. castor sugar	

Coconut cake

you will need:

6 oz. self-raising flour	3 eggs
pinch salt	¼ teaspoon vanilla essence
1 level teaspoon baking	2 oz. desiccated coconut
powder	about 4 tablespoons milk
6 oz. castor sugar	
6 oz. margarine	

The cooking time for each of these cakes is 20 minutes. Bake in a moderately hot oven (375° F.—Mark 5) on the third shelf from the top.

Method of making quick mix cakes

1 Grease two 8-inch sandwich tins and line the bottom of each with a round of greaseproof paper.
2 Chop up the margarine in a mixing bowl.
3 Sieve in the dry ingredients.
4 Add the sugar, eggs, essence or flavouring and the milk.
5 Beat well for 1 minute until evenly mixed, adding another spoonful of milk if necessary to make a dropping consistency.
6 Spread the mixture into the two tins.
7 Bake until firm then turn on to a wire tray to cool.
8 When cold, sandwich with butter cream and ice and decorate as liked.

Special Occasion Cakes

Birthday or Christening cake

cooking time 4½ - 5 hours

you will need:

8 oz. butter	8 oz. currants
8 oz. brown sugar	8 oz. raisins
4 eggs	3 oz. glacé cherries
8 oz. plain flour	3 oz. candied peel
pinch salt	2 oz. blanched almonds
¼ teaspoon spice	3 tablespoons lemon juice
½ teaspoon nutmeg	grated rind 1 lemon
8 oz. sultanas	3 - 4 tablespoons brandy
	(optional)

1 Grease and line a 7-inch square or 8-inch round tin with a double thickness of greased greaseproof paper.
2 Sieve flour, salt and spices.
3 Cream the butter and sugar together until light and fluffy. Beat the eggs into the creamed mixture.
4 Fold in the sieved flour. Add the lemon juice and rind.
5 Stir in the prepared fruit and nuts, mix all well together and put into the tin.
6 Bake in a slow oven (290° F.—Mark 1). Allow cake to cool before removing from tin.
7 Prick base of the cake and pour over the brandy. When cold, wrap in greaseproof or foil and store in an airtight tin until required.
8 Cover with almond paste.
9 Coat with royal icing and decorate.

Anniversary cake

cooking time 5 - 5½ hours

you will need:

8 oz. flour	finely grated rind
4 oz. fine semolina	1 medium orange
1 level teaspoon mixed	8 oz. each currants and
spice	sultanas, washed and
¼ level teaspoon each	dried
nutmeg and cinnamon	4 oz. dates, finely chopped
1 tablespoon instant	4 oz. glacé cherries,
coffee powder	quartered
pinch salt	2 oz. chopped mixed peel
8 oz. butter or margarine	2 oz. walnuts or blanched
8 oz. soft brown sugar	almonds, finely chopped
4 large eggs	4 oz. seedless raisins,
2 level tablespoons golden	washed and dried
syrup	

1 Grease and line an 8- or 9-inch round cake tin.
2 Sieve the dry ingredients together.
3 Cream the fat and sugar until light and fluffy.
4 Add the eggs, one at a time, beating thoroughly after each addition.
5 Stir in the syrup, half the dry ingredients, the orange rind and all the fruit and nuts. Mix thoroughly.
6 Stir in the remaining flour, then turn mixture into the prepared tin.
7 Bake in the centre of a cool oven (290° F.—Mark 1).
8 Leave in the tin for at least 30 minutes, then turn out on to a wire tray and remove the paper.

Rich fruit cake

cooking time 4 - 4½ hours

you will need:

8 oz. soft brown sugar	1 lb. currants
8 oz. butter	8 oz. raisins
5 eggs	8 oz. sultanas
10 oz. flour	4 oz. glacé cherries,
½ oz. mixed spice	chopped
¾ teaspoon lemon essence	4 oz. chopped mixed peel
½ teaspoon almond essence	rum, brandy or sherry for
1 tablespoon black treacle	steeping the fruit and for
or marmalade	pouring over the cake

1 Grease and line a 9-inch cake tin. Tie folded brown paper or newspaper round the outside of the tin.
2 Put all the fruit into a bowl and pour a wine-glass of spirit over it. Leave overnight.
3 Sieve the flour and spice.
4 Cream the fat and sugar until light and fluffy. Add the essence, treacle or marmalade.
5 Gradually beat in the eggs.
6 Lightly fold in half the flour. Mix the remaining flour with the fruit. Stir into the cake mixture.
7 Turn mixture into the tin and make a shallow hollow in the centre.
8 Place a pad of newspaper in the oven on the middle shelf. Bake the cake at 335° F.—Mark 3 for 1 hour. Reduce to 310° F.—Mark 2 for the next hour, then reduce to 290° F.—Mark 1 for the remaining cooking time.
9 Turn the cake out on to a wire tray. Remove the paper. Prick the bottom of the cake and pour a little spirit over.
10 When the cake is cold, wrap it in foil or greaseproof paper and store until required. Make the cake 6 - 8 weeks before it is required.

Light fruit cake

cooking time 2½ - 3 hours

you will need:

8 oz. butter	6 oz. glacé pineapple,
8 oz. castor sugar	chopped
4 large eggs	4 oz. candied peel,
12 oz. flour	chopped
pinch salt	4 oz. walnuts, chopped
1 level teaspoon baking	grated rind 1 lemon
powder	juice ¼ lemon
6 oz. stem ginger, drained	
and chopped	

1 Grease and line an 8-inch round cake tin.
2 Sieve flour, salt and baking powder.
3 Cream butter and sugar until light and fluffy.
4 Beat in the eggs gradually.
5 Fold in the flour.
6 Add the fruit, nuts, rind and juice. Mix gently.
7 Turn mixture into cake tin. Bake at 325° F.— Mark 3 covering cake with paper during last hour.

8 Remove cake from tin, strip off paper and leave on a wire tray until cold.
9 Cover cake with almond paste and royal icing.

Almond paste

you will need:

12 oz. ground almonds	2 or 3 drops almond
6 oz. castor sugar	essence
6 oz. icing sugar	2 eggs

1 Sieve the icing sugar.
2 Mix the ground almonds, castor and icing sugar together.
3 Add the essence and the eggs.
4 Knead until well mixed and smooth.

To cover a cake with almond paste

1 Trim the cake if necessary, making the top flat. Brush off any crumbs.
2 Brush the top of the cake with warmed apricot jam.
3 Cut almond paste in half, roll out on a surface sprinkled with castor sugar into a round ¼ inch thick, the same size as the top of the cake.
4 Turn the cake upside-down. Place on the round of almond paste and press down firmly. Trim the edge of the almond paste if necessary. Turn cake upright again.
5 Measure the sides of the cake. Roll out remaining paste into a strip of this length and width. Brush the strip with warmed apricot jam.
6 Press the strip in position against the side of the cake, making a neat join. Roll a jam jar firmly over the top and around sides of the cake. The strip of paste can be cut in one or two pieces for easier handling.
7 Allow the almond paste to dry out for 2 - 3 days in a cool place before icing the cake.

Royal icing

you will need:

1 lb. icing sugar	1 teaspoon lemon juice
2 egg whites	½ teaspoon glycerine

1 Leave the egg whites in a cool place overnight.
2 Sieve the icing sugar.
3 Whisk the egg whites until frothy.
4 Beat in half the icing sugar, add the lemon juice and glycerine.
5 Continue beating in the sugar until the icing can be drawn into stiff peaks.

6 Scrape the icing down from the sides of the bowl. Cover with a damp cloth and use as required.

Guide to amount of almond icing and royal icing required for covering rich fruit cakes

Size of cake

7-inch round	$1\frac{1}{4}$ lb. almond paste and royal icing
7-inch square	$1\frac{1}{2}$ lb. almond paste and royal icing
8-inch round	$1\frac{3}{4}$ lb. almond paste and royal icing
8-inch square	2 lb. almond paste and royal icing
9-inch round	2 lb. almond paste and royal icing
9-inch square	$2\frac{1}{4}$ lb. almond paste and royal icing

To pipe icing on a cake

Have ready an icing pipe and forcing bag. Choose a writing pipe for making lines and dots, for scalloped edgings and words, a star pipe for rosettes, ropes or coils or for zig-zag lines or a shell pipe for a firm, well-defined edge. The forcing bag may be bought, nylon or fabric, or it may be made of greaseproof paper.

To make a forcing bag

1 Cut a 10-inch square of greaseproof paper diagonally across to form two triangles. Shape each triangle into a cone as illustrated.
2 Bring the three points together and hold firmly between thumb and forefinger.
3 Secure the three points together with a paper clip or by folding the paper over several times.
4 Cut off a small piece, about $\frac{1}{2}$ inch, from the point of the cone and drop in the icing pipe. About $\frac{1}{4}$ inch of the pipe should protrude. Spoon some icing into the bag, fold the top of the bag over once or twice. Hold the bag with both hands, thumbs in the centre, resting on the top to control the pressure.
To pipe icing on a cake, work with the pipe held close to the surface of the cake but not touching it, and work from the centre of the top outwards. If several pipes are used in the design, or more than one colour of icing is used, have several bags ready with pipes in position before starting to decorate the cake.

Wedding cake

cooking time $3\frac{3}{4}$ - $6\frac{3}{4}$ hours

you will need:

$1\frac{1}{4}$ lb. currants	10 oz. ground almonds
$1\frac{1}{4}$ lb. sultanas	$1\frac{1}{4}$ lb. flour
$1\frac{1}{4}$ lb. raisins	$\frac{1}{2}$ teaspoon salt
10 oz. cherries	$2\frac{1}{2}$ teaspoons nutmeg
10 oz. peel	$2\frac{1}{2}$ teaspoons mixed spice
$1\frac{1}{2}$ lb. butter	$2\frac{1}{2}$ teaspoons cinnamon
$1\frac{1}{2}$ lb. sugar	10 lb. almond paste
2 lemons	10 lb. icing sugar
12 eggs	

1 Grease 3 round tins 10, 8 and 6 inches and line each with a double thickness of greased grease-proof paper.
2 Prepare the fruit. Chop the cherries and peel.
3 Sieve flour, salt and spices into a large bowl (clean washing-up bowl may be used).
4 Mix all the prepared fruit with the sieved flour.
5 Grate the lemon rind very finely.
6 Cream the butter and sugar until white and shiny.
7 Beat in the lemon rind.
8 Beat in the eggs one at a time, adding a little of the ground almonds after each egg.
9 Lightly stir in the fruit and flour mixture and any remaining almonds.
10 Divide the mixture among the three tins and bake in a slow oven (290° F.—Mark 1). Allow $3\frac{3}{4}$ - 4 hours for the 6-inch tin, $4\frac{1}{2}$ - $4\frac{3}{4}$ hours for the 8-inch tin and $6\frac{1}{4}$ - $6\frac{3}{4}$ hours for the 10-inch tin.
11 Remove the cakes from the oven as each is cooked and allow to cool in the tin for at least 10 minutes. Turn on to a wire tray, strip off the greaseproof paper.
12 Prick the surface of each cake with a fine skewer or needle. Pour 3 - 4 tablespoons brandy over each and leave to soak in.
13 When the cakes are completely cold, wrap each in foil and store in a cool dry place for at least 3 weeks or up to 3 months.
If preferred, the cake may be made in two stages. Use half the quantity for the large tin and divide the remaining mixture between the two smaller tins. The whole mixture may be prepared and cooked separately. Leave the cakes in a cool place until ready to go into the oven.
Half this mixture may be used to make a 10-inch round or a 9-inch square cake suitable for a 21st birthday cake.

Icing and decorating the wedding cake

1 Brush each cake with apricot glaze (see foot of column 2). Cover with almond paste and leave to dry out for at least one week before applying the first coat of icing.
2 Coat each cake with stiff royal icing and leave to harden for at least 2 days, making sure it is protected from dust.
3 Coat the cakes a second time, making the royal icing slightly thinner (so that it will coat the back of a spoon).
4 When the cakes are dry, fix each to a board using a generous amount of royal icing. Use a board at least 1 inch larger than the iced cake.
5 Using a round cutter, lightly mark semi-circles round the edge of each cake, about 1 inch down from the top of the cake, making a scalloped edge effect.
6 Pipe the scallop round each cake using royal icing and a writing tube. Leave to dry.
7 Using a No. 12 nozzle, pipe a raised edge round the top and base of each cake. Leave to dry.
8 When the cake is required, place one tier on top of the other. Decorate with fresh, home-made or bought flowers, silver leaves and ribbon.
  If preferred the tiers may be supported by pillars. Use four 3-inch pillars on the bottom tier to support the 8-inch cake and four 4-inch pillars to support the 6-inch cake.
  The flowers may be arranged in a silver vase on the top tier if preferred.

Dundee cake

cooking time 3 hours

you will need:

2 oz. almonds	8 oz. butter
2 oz. glacé cherries	8 oz. castor sugar
4 oz. candied peel	grated rind ½ lemon
8 oz. currants	4 eggs
8 oz. sultanas	8 oz. flour
2 oz. cornflour	1 level teaspoon baking powder

1 Grease and line an 8-inch cake tin.
2 Blanch the almonds, chop 1 oz. and split the remainder.
3 Wash and chop the cherries and peel. Clean the currants and sultanas if necessary.
4 Put all the fruit and chopped almonds in a bowl and coat well with the cornflour.
5 Cream the butter and sugar, adding the lemon rind.
6 Beat in the eggs, one at a time.

7 Sieve the flour and baking powder, fold into the creamed mixture.
8 Lightly stir in the fruit coated with cornflour.
9 Put the mixture into the prepared tin.
10 Bake in a slow oven (310° F.—Mark 2). Arrange the split almonds on top of the cake after it has been in the oven for 30 minutes.

Cherry cake

cooking time 1½ hours

you will need:

6 oz. margarine	6 oz. flour
6 oz. castor sugar	2 oz. ground almonds
3 eggs	6 oz. glacé cherries

1 Grease and line a 7-inch cake tin.
2 Sieve the flour and add the ground almonds.
3 Halve the washed, dried cherries and mix with the flour.
4 Cream the fat and sugar and beat in the eggs.
5 Fold in the flour mixture.
6 Turn into the prepared tin and bake at 335° F. —Mark 3.

Almonds

To blanch: put into cold water. Bring almost to boiling point. Pour away the hot water and cover the almonds with cold. Rub in a soft cloth and pinch off the skins. Almonds for decoration are usually split lengthways and used rounded side up. To give them a good shine, brush with egg white and dry off in the oven.

Toasted almonds

Blanch the almonds. Place on a baking sheet and place in a moderate oven or under the grill until golden. Turn frequently. When cold store in a jar until required. Almonds may be tossed in a little melted butter before browning. Drain well on kitchen paper, but do not store.

Apricot glaze

you will need:

4 tablespoons apricot jam	lemon juice (optional)
2 tablespoons water	

1 Sieve the apricot jam into a small pan.
2 Add the water and bring to the boil.
3 Add lemon juice to taste, if liked.
  Use to glaze small cakes and for brushing cakes before applying almond paste.

Party time gâteau

cooking time 20 minutes

you will need:

3 eggs	glacé icing made with
4 oz. castor sugar	5 oz. icing sugar
3 oz. flour	2 oz. walnuts or desiccated
2 oz. butter	coconut
butter cream made with	
4 oz. butter (see page 80)	

1 Grease and line the bottom of 3 7-inch sandwich tins.
2 Sieve the flour and put it in a warm place until required.
3 Melt the butter and allow it to cool slightly.
4 Whisk the eggs and sugar together in a basin over a pan of hot water until thick enough to hold the mark of the whisk.
5 Remove from hot water and continue whisking until mixture is cool.
6 Lightly pour the butter into the mixture.
7 Fold in the flour at the same time folding in the butter.
8 When the butter and flour are evenly mixed through the whisked eggs and sugar, pour into the prepared tins.
9 Bake at 375° F.—Gas Mark 5—until well risen and golden.
10 Allow to cool for three to five minutes, carefully loosen round the sides and turn out on to a wire tray.
11 When cold, sandwich the cakes together with some of the butter cream, spread butter cream round the sides of the cake. Roll the sides of the cake in desiccated coconut or crushed walnuts.
12 Pour glacé icing over the top of the cake. Leave to set.
13 Decorate with piped butter icing, candles, etc., as liked.

Orange dream cake

cooking time 50 minutes

you will need:

2 eggs	*Frosting:*
5 tablespoons corn oil	1 egg white
1 large orange	4 oz. castor sugar
6 oz. plain flour	1 tablespoon water
2 level teaspoons baking	juice and grated rind
powder	$\frac{1}{2}$ orange
$\frac{1}{2}$ level teaspoon salt	crystallised orange slices
5 oz. castor sugar	angelica

1 Grease a 7-inch tube or ring tin.
2 Separate the yolks and whites of the eggs.
3 Squeeze the juice from the orange and make up to 5 tablespoons with water.
4 Mix together the egg yolks, oil and orange juice.

5 Sieve the flour, baking powder and salt, and add with the sugar, to the yolks, oil and orange juice.
6 Beat well together to form a smooth batter.
7 Whisk egg whites until stiff, fold into the mixture.
8 Turn into the tin.
9 Bake in a moderate oven (350° F.—Gas Mark 4) until risen and firm to the touch.
10 Turn out on to a wire tray and leave until cold.
11 Cover cake with frosting and decorate with orange slices and diamonds cut from strips of angelica.
12 To make the frosting, mix together egg white, sugar, water and orange juice. Whisk over hot water until icing becomes fluffy and stands in peaks. Stir in orange rind.

Rose and star cake

1 Cover an 8-inch round cake with white, royal or fondant icing. Place on a board and leave to dry.
2 Draw a 6-pointed star on thin card or stiff paper. Cut out shape and place in the centre of the cake.
3 Prick round the outline with a needle or a very fine skewer, then remove the shape.
4 Using a No. 1 writing tube and royal icing, pipe the shape of the star following the pricked outline.
5 Fill the star with pastel tinted glacé icing or, royal icing thinned with lemon juice. Use a fine brush or tip of a knife to ease the icing into the points. Leave to dry.
6 Make a cluster of small roses and leaves (bought or made of icing and almond paste) in the centre of the star, sticking them into position with a little royal icing.
7 Pipe a shell edge using a No. 12 nozzle and white royal icing, around the base of the cake where it joins the board. Decorate with small sprays of roses and leaves, working from the shell edge up the sides of the cake.

Star Christmas cake

Prepare the cake as above. Stud the star outline with silver balls or fill the star with silver balls. Fix a candle in a holder in the centre of the star and decorate with red ribbon and holly. Pipe shell edge around the base, stud with silver balls and arrange holly leaves about 2 inches apart on the shell edge.

Icings and Fillings

Butter cream

you will need:

4 oz. butter   vanilla essence
6 - 8 oz. icing sugar

1 Sieve the icing sugar.
2 Beat butter with a wooden spoon or spatula until soft.
3 Beat icing sugar into the butter, adding a few drops of vanilla essence.
The amount of icing sugar needed will depend on the consistency of the cream required.

Orange or lemon butter cream

Add finely-grated lemon or orange rind and juice to taste to the creamed butter and sugar. Beat hard to prevent curdling.

Walnut butter cream

Add 2 tablespoons finely chopped walnuts to creamed butter and sugar and mix in thoroughly.

Almond butter cream

Add 2 tablespoons finely chopped toasted almonds to creamed butter and sugar.

Coffee butter cream

Make as basic butter cream, adding the vanilla essence and 2 teaspoons coffee essence.

Mocha butter cream

Make as coffee butter cream, adding 2 oz. melted chocolate as well as the coffee essence.

Chocolate butter cream

Melt a 2 oz. bar plain chocolate. Beat 2 oz. butter until soft. Blend in the melted chocolate and 3 oz. sieved icing sugar.

Coffee essence

Blend 3 tablespoons instant coffee with 2 tablespoons lemon juice or rum. Dissolve 8 oz. sugar in ¾ pint water and bring to the boil. Boil for 10 minutes. Pour the boiling syrup on to the coffee mixture, stirring. When cold, pour into a screw-top bottle and store in a cool place. Use as required.

Glacé icing

you will need:

8 oz. icing sugar   flavouring and colouring
2 - 3 tablespoons warm   as liked
   water

1 Sieve the icing sugar into a bowl, using a wooden spoon to press sugar through sieve if necessary.
2 Add water gradually, beating well until icing is smooth and glossy and of a good coating consistency, i.e. will coat the back of a spoon.
3 Add flavouring and colouring and blend it well into the mixture.
If icing is required only for the top of the cake it should be slightly thicker so that it can be spread out smoothly and be kept to the edge.

Lemon or orange glacé icing

Make as above, using 2 tablespoons lemon juice or orange juice instead of water and add 2 - 3 drops orange or lemon colouring.

Coffee glacé icing

Make as above, reducing the amount of water by 2 teaspoons and using 2 teaspoons coffee essence.

Chocolate glacé icing

Melt 2 oz. plain chocolate in a small bowl over a pan of hot water. Blend in 4 oz. sieved icing sugar and 1 tablespoon water. For extra gloss, add 2 - 3 drops oil.

Chocolate icing

Break a 4 oz. bar of chocolate into a small bowl over a pan of hot water. Heat gently until the chocolate has melted, taking care that the water does not boil. Add a few drops of water and olive oil if liked to give a thin glossy coating icing.

Chocolate frosting

Melt 6 oz. plain chocolate in a bowl over hot water. Stir in 12 oz. sieved icing sugar and blend in 6 tablespoons evaporated milk. Beat until smooth. Allow to cool, beat again and spread over cake or cakes as liked.

Feather icing

Cover cake with glacé icing. Before the icing sets, pipe lines (with a writing pipe) of icing in a contrasting colour across the cake. Run a knife across the cake in the opposite direction, cutting through the lines of icing at right angles. Work quickly, using a light pressure on the knife making the 'lines' about ½ inch apart.

Fondant icing

you will need:

2 lb. loaf or granulated sugar	4 oz. glucose or a good 3 or 4 drops lemon juice
½ pint water	

1 Dissolve the sugar in the water over a low heat.
2 Add the glucose and lemon juice, bring to the boil quickly.
3 Continue boiling until a temperature of 240° F. is reached.
4 Pour on to a marble slab, brushed with oil or water, and leave to cool until a skin begins to form round the edge.
5 Work the icing syrup backwards and forwards with a spatula or palette knife until it becomes firm and opaque. Keep the mixture together as much as possible.
6 Knead the icing by hand until of an even texture throughout.
7 Use at once, or wrap in greaseproof paper and store in a cool place until required.
8 To use after storing, heat in a basin over a pan of hot water, stirring until the consistency of thick cream. Allow to cool.

If a slab is not available, the icing can be 'worked' in a large bowl.

Fondant icing may be used as a foundation for royal or glacé icing in place of almond paste. When used in this way, it may be flavoured with almond essence and it may also be mixed with desiccated coconut. It can also be used for coating rich cakes with or without fruit.

Scraps of fondant icing can be kept and used to make decorations for iced cakes, flowers and fruit, etc.

To ice a cake with fondant

Have the cake covered with almond paste a few days beforehand to allow the paste to dry out.

1 Brush the surface of almond paste with egg white.
2 Dust rolling pin and working surface with sieved icing sugar.
3 Roll the fondant out, at least ¼ inch thick. Lift on to the cake using the rolling pin.
4 Dust the palms of the hands with sieved icing sugar and smooth the icing over the top of the cake, working it down the sides and making sure that the corners are neat.
5 Trim off the uneven icing from the base of the cake.
6 Have cake board ready, also some royal icing made up, if the cake is to be stuck into position.
7 Lift the cake with two fish slices or palette knives and place on the board.

If the cake is to be 'stuck' on to the board, roughly spread royal icing over the board before placing the cake in position.

Seven minute frosting

you will need:

2 lb. loaf or granulated sugar	4 tablespoons water large pinch cream of tartar colouring (optional)
½ pint water	

1 Put all the ingredients in a bowl and whisk lightly.
2 Place bowl over hot water and continue whisking until mixture thickens sufficiently to hold in peaks.
3 Tint with a few drops of colouring if liked.

Chocolate frosting

you will need:

4 oz. plain chocolate	2 egg yolks
½ oz. butter	4 tablespoons milk
4 oz. icing sugar, sieved	½ teaspoon vanilla essence

1 Melt the chocolate in a bowl over hot water.
2 Add butter, beat in remaining ingredients.
3 Whisk mixture until it will thickly coat the back of a spoon.
4 Swirl over cake.

American frosting

you will need:

1 lb. loaf sugar	pinch cream of tartar
¼ pint water	2 egg whites

1 Dissolve the sugar in the water. Add a pinch of cream of tartar and boil rapidly until mixture reaches temperature of 240° F.
2 Whisk the egg whites until stiff.
3 Pour sugar syrup in a thin stream on to the egg whites and continue whisking until mixture thickens sufficiently to hold in peaks.
4 Spread quickly over the cake.

Creamy frosting

you will need:

4 oz. butter	2 tablespoons water
1 lb. icing sugar	1 egg white
pinch salt	colouring (optional)
1 teaspoon vanilla essence	

1 Sieve the icing sugar and salt.
2 Beat the butter until really soft and gradually work in one-third of the sugar.
3 Add the vanilla essence and water and beat until well blended.
4 Beat in half the remaining sugar, then the egg white.
5 Gradually beat in the remaining sugar until the icing is the consistency required. If the icing is difficult to beat at any stage, add a little lemon juice or water.
6 Add colouring if liked.

Mock cream

you will need:

4 oz. butter	3 tablespoons boiling water
4 oz. castor sugar	2 tablespoons cold milk

1 Cream the butter and sugar until light in colour and shiny.
2 Beat in the boiling water a drop at a time.
3 Gradually add the milk in the same way.
4 Leave in a cold place until firm.

Continental cream

you will need:

$\frac{1}{2}$ pint cream	$1\frac{1}{2}$ oz. icing sugar
1 - 2 egg yolks	$\frac{1}{2}$ teaspoon vanilla essence

1 Sieve the icing sugar.
2 Whisk the cream until thick.
3 Beat the egg yolks with the sugar, adding the vanilla essence.
4 Fold the yolk mixture into the cream, mixing thoroughly.

Vienna icing

you will need:

2 oz. butter	2 tablespoons sherry
6 oz. icing sugar	colouring (optional)

1 Sieve the icing sugar.
2 Beat the butter until soft, gradually adding the icing sugar.

3 Add the sherry and continue beating until the icing is smooth.
4 Add colouring if liked.

Orange Vienna icing

Make as above, adding 1 level teaspoon grated orange rind.

Chocolate Vienna icing

Make as above, replacing 1 tablespoon icing sugar with one of cocoa.

Chocolate filling

Blend 2 oz. butter with 2 oz. melted chocolate, cooled. Beat in 2 oz. ground almonds and 2 oz. sugar.

Chocolate rum filling

Make as above, adding rum or rum essence to taste.

Rum and walnut filling

Cream 2 oz. butter with 3 oz. brown sugar. Gradually beat in 2 dessertspoons rum to taste. Stir in 2 oz. chopped walnuts.

Coconut filling

Blend 2 oz. sieved icing sugar with 1 egg yolk and 1 tablespoon lemon juice. Heat gently in a basin over a pan of hot water until thick—about 5 minutes. Remove from the heat, stir in 1 oz. desiccated coconut. Allow to cool before using.

Cream filling

Blend $\frac{1}{2}$ oz. cornflour with a little milk, taken from $\frac{1}{4}$ pint. Bring the rest to the boil. Pour on to the blended cornflour, stirring. Return the mixture to the pan. Cook for 3 minutes, stirring throughout. Leave to cool. Cream 1 oz. butter with 1 oz. sugar. Gradually beat the cornflour mixture. Beat well, add 2 - 3 drops vanilla essence. Allow to become cold before using.

A Party - Chinese Style

Chinese food is wonderful food for a party. Not only is it still enormously popular to eat, but a Chinese meal provides such a good theme for simple decorations, with lanterns and streamers setting the scene. Most people are interested in the Chinese way of preparing food and find the combination of sweet and sour, and the clever use of contrasting texture so intriguing that this will provide a good topic of conversation at the table. The added advantage of this kind of party food is that it is not difficult to cook; the preparation takes some time but all the work can be done beforehand and the last-minute cooking is done very quickly. Provide three or four savoury dishes, plenty of rice and a mixed salad, if possible have some way of keeping the dishes hot on the table so that guests can help themselves throughout the meal. Lychees or preserved ginger, with or without cream, is all that is required for dessert; pineapple is refreshing too, after well-seasoned dishes.

After the meal serve hot China tea, without milk or sugar, accompanied by rice cakes. For a really authentic atmosphere you can buy Chinese serving dishes and chopsticks at a reasonable price from most Chinese restaurants and stores which sell Chinese food.

Beef with fried noodles

cooking time 20 minutes

you will need:

8 oz. minced beef	$\frac{1}{2}$ pint beef stock
1 small onion	2 level teaspoons
1 clove garlic	cornflour
2 sticks celery	2 teaspoons soy sauce
$\frac{1}{2}$ green pepper	pinch taste powder
3 tomatoes	3 oz. dry noodles
1 - 2 tablespoons oil	oil for deep frying

1 Chop onion and garlic finely.
2 Sauté in hot oil with minced beef, until the meat is browned.
3 Chop celery, pepper and tomatoes roughly.
4 Add vegetables to meat, stir in stock, simmer for 10 minutes.
5 Blend cornflour and taste powder with soy sauce and a little cold water.
6 Stir into meat mixture and cook gently for 3 minutes.
7 Serve with fried noodles.

Fried rice

cooking time 1 hour

you will need:

4 oz. Patna rice	$\frac{1}{2}$ level teaspoon salt
2 tablespoons oil	4 oz. prawns or shrimps
$\frac{3}{4}$ pint water	$\frac{1}{2}$ green pepper

1 Fry the rice in the oil until golden, about 10 minutes.
2 Add half the water, simmer gently until all the water is absorbed.
3 Add the rest of the water and salt to taste.
4 Cut the pepper into strips, add to the rice and continue cooking over a gentle heat for 30 minutes.
5 Stir in prawns or shrimps, and cook until heated through, stirring with a fork thoughout.

To fry noodles

Cook noodles in boiling salted water until tender—about 15 minutes. Drain well. Fry in deep oil at 375° F. for 5 minutes until crisp and brown. Drain on absorbent paper, serve very hot.

Taste powder

There are several brands of taste powder (or monosodium glutamate) available in this country. Taste powders do not add to the seasoning in the dish, but bring out the natural flavours.

Prawn and Pork balls

cooking time 10 minutes

you will need:

6 oz. shelled prawns, fresh,	1 teaspoon sugar
frozen or canned	1 tablespoon sherry
6 oz. pork	2 tablespoons soy sauce
1 level tablespoon cornflour	2 tablespoons oil
1 level teaspoon salt	

1 Mince the prawns and pork together.
2 Blend the cornflour, sugar, salt, sherry and soy sauce.
3 Mix sauce mixture with minced prawns and pork.
4 Form into small balls, press flat into rounds about $\frac{1}{2}$ inch thick.
5 Sauté in hot oil until well cooked and brown, about 5 minutes on each side.
6 Drain and serve very hot.

Pork with bamboo shoots

cooking time 25 minutes

you will need:

8 oz. pork	1 teaspoon Chinese hot
1 10-oz. can bamboo shoots	sauce
2 - 3 tablespoons oil	2 tablespoons sherry
4 tablespoons beef stock	I level teaspoon
	cornflour
	½ level teaspoon salt

1 Cut the pork and bamboo shoots into small pieces.
2 Heat 2 tablespoons oil in a frying pan, fry bamboo shoots for 3 minutes. Drain.
3 Blend sauce, sherry, cornflour and salt.
4 Coat pork in sauce mixture.
5 Add remaining oil to the frying pan if necessary, sauté pork for 10 - 15 minutes until cooked through.
6 Replace bamboo shoots in pan, add stock and cook for a further 5 minutes.

Chop suey

cooking time 40 minutes

you will need:

8 oz. lean meat, beef or	½ firm cabbage
pork	2 medium onions
2 level tablespoons	2 small carrots
cornflour	1 small can bean sprouts
3 tablespoons oil	2 tomatoes
salt and pepper	2 oz. bamboo shoots
½ pint chicken stock	4 oz. mushrooms

1 Cut the meat into small pieces, toss in corn-flour, seasoned with a pinch of salt and pepper.
2 Brown the meat in 2 tablespoons of oil in a large pan. Add the stock.
3 Slice the cabbage finely, chop onions, slice carrots.
4 Sauté in remaining oil in a separate pan.
5 Add remaining vegetables cut into small pieces, toss together and cook for further 5 minutes.
6 Add all vegetables to meat, cover and cook over a gentle heat until the meat is tender.

Chicken chow mein

cooking time 20 minutes

you will need:

½ small onion	½ pint chicken stock
2 sticks celery	10 water chestnuts
2 oz. mushrooms	1 small can bean sprouts
1 - 2 tablespoons oil	1 level tablespoon
½ lb. cooked chicken	cornflour
	1 tablespoon soy sauce

1 Slice onion, chop celery, slice mushrooms, sauté in hot oil.
2 Dice chicken, add to vegetables.

3 Pour in stock and simmer for 5 minutes.
4 Slice chestnuts, add to chicken, with bean sprouts.
5 Blend cornflour with same and stir in, cook for a further 5 minutes and serve.

Sweet and sour pork

cooking time 30 minutes

you will need:

1 lb. cooked pork	1 dessertspoon made
¼ pint vinegar	mustard
4 oz. sugar	1 small green pepper
1 level tablespoon	1 small red pepper
cornflour	1 small can pineapple
1 dessertspoon Worcester-	chunks
shire sauce	salt

1 Cut the pork into strips.
2 Heat the vinegar and sugar over a gentle heat until the sugar is dissolved.
3 Blend the cornflour to a smooth paste with a little cold water.
4 Add to the vinegar, bring to the boil, cook until thick and clear, stirring.
5 Add the pineapple cubes and ¼ pint of the juice.
6 Add sauce and mustard, and peppers cut into strips or rings.
7 Cover and simmer for 15 minutes.
8 Add the pork and continue to cook until heated through.

Chinese rice cakes

cooking time 20 minutes

you will need:

4 oz. flour	3 oz. lard
1 oz. ground rice	1 egg
½ oz. cornflour	1 tablespoon water
3 oz. castor sugar	¼ teaspoon almond
pinch salt	essence
½ level teaspoon baking	few blanched almonds
powder	

1 Sieve the flour, rice, cornflour, sugar, salt and baking powder into a bowl.
2 Rub in the lard until the mixture looks like breadcrumbs.
3 Add ½ the egg, beaten, water and essence and mix to a smooth dough.
4 Form dough into small balls, place on a greased baking tray.
5 Press an almond on the top of each cake, brush with remaining egg.
6 Bake in a moderately hot oven (375° F.—Gas Mark 5) for 15 - 20 minutes.
7 Cool on a wire tray.

Index

Honey:
Honey chocolate icing, 29
Honeybee biscuits, 35
Hors-d'oeuvre, 48
Hostess casserole, 17
Hot cheese dip, 21
Hot dogs, 20
Hot mushroom dip, 21
Hot soufflés, 65

I

ICE CREAM:
Dairy ice cream, 38
Iced coffee, 8
Ice cream sauces, 38
Iced rings, 34

ICINGS AND FROSTINGS:
Guide to amount of icings required, 76
To make an icing forcing bag, 76
To pipe icing, 76
American frosting, 81
Chocolate frosting, 80
Chocolate icing, 80
Chocolate Vienna icing, 82
Coffee glacé icing, 80
Cream frosting, 82
Feather icing, 81
Fondant icing, 81
Glacé icing, 80
Honey chocolate icing, 29
Lemon or orange icing, 80
Orange Vienna icing, 82
Royal icing, 76
Seven minute frosting, 81
Vienna icing, 82
Imperial stars, 14

J

JAM:
Jam or lemon curd tartlets, 34
Jam pancakes, 65
Jam puffs, 70
Java mocha, 8

K

KEBABS:
Kebabs, 22
Steak and mushroom kebabs, 26
King size sausage rolls, 24

L

Lamb:
Lamb chops and mushrooms, 54
Lamb en brochette, 26
Lemon:
Lemon cake dessert, 20
Lemon coconut cookies, 31
Lemon cream, 31
Lemon cream jelly, 38
Lemon fish casserole, 52
Lemon German biscuits, 45
Lemon hearts, 70
Lemon layer cake (quick mix), 74
Lemon meringue pie, 61
Lemon or orange glacé icing, 80
Lemon sponge fingers, 45
Light fruit cake, 76
Lime mousse, 46
Lobster mayonnaise, 53
Lobster quiche, 16

M

Macaroons, 45
Madeleines, 36
Maids of honour, 70
Maître d'hôtel butter, 47
Mandarin:
Mandarin gâteau, 24
Mandarin trifle, 46
Marguerites, 42
Marzipan petits fours, 30

MAYONNAISE:
Cooked mayonnaise, 60
Lobster mayonnaise, 53
Mayonnaise, 60
Salmon mayonnaise, 53

Index

Steak:
Austrian steak, 55
Grilled steak, 48
Steak and cheeseburgers, 22
Steak and kidney pie, 55
Steak and mushroom kebabs, 26
Steamed cucumbers, 58
Strawberry meringue gâteau, 24
Strawberry mousse, 63
Strawberry shortcake, 63
Stuffed breast of veal, 55
Stuffed celery sticks, 43
Stuffed loin of pork, 56
Sugar biscuits, 36
Summer pudding, 62
Sweet dreams, 37
Sweet and sour pork, 84
Swiss cream, 62
Swiss roll, 72
Swiss tarts, 36
Syrup tartlets, 34

T

TARTLETS, see CAKES
TARTS:
Canadian apple tart, 71
Florentine tart, 71
Frangipane tart, 71
Taste powder, 83
Tea scones, 68
Teenage party, 20
Tipsy cakes, 19
Toffee apples, 37

Tomatoes:
Baked tomatoes, 47
Tomato salad, 48
Tomato soup, 50
Traffic light biscuits, 35

Trout:
Smoked trout, 49
Truffle cakes, 30

Tuna:
Tuna coleslaw, 50
Tuna flan, 16

Turkey:
To cook, 40

V

Veal:
Casserole of veal, 54
Stuffed breast of veal, 55
Veal with tomatoes and spaghetti, 56
Wiener schnitzel, 55

Vegetables:
Mixed vegetables, conservatively cooked, 57
Victoria sandwich, 73
Vienna icing, 82
Viennese fingers, 45
Viennese shortcakes, 45
Viennese tartlets, 45
Virginia salad, 18

VOLS-AU-VENT:
To make vols-au-vent (bouchées), 42
Fillings for vols-au-vent (bouchées), 42

W

Walnut butter cream, 80

Watercress:
Watercress butter, 48
Watercress and potato soup, 51
Wedding cake, 77
Wedding reception, 40
Western style chops, 54
White sauce, 59
White wine cup, 7
Wiener schnitzel, 55

WINES:
To choose wines, 7
White wine cup, 7
Wine punch, 8